ADVANCE PRAISE

"Women face more than a few unique sleep challenges and Shelby Harris has provided a straightforward, comprehensive, and much-needed resource to explain what's going on and, more importantly, what to do about it. She expertly guides the reader through state-of-the-art treatment for insomnia using her clinical experience to illustrate how even the trickiest situations can be conquered."

—Janet Krone Kennedy, Ph.D., author of *The Good Sleeper: The Essential Guide to Sleep for Your Baby (and You)* and founder of NYC Sleep Doctor

"Dr. Harris's book is an important contribution to our understanding of the unique and often overlooked issues related to insomnia in women. A range of hormonal and lifestyle changes over the course of women's lives negatively affect their sleep patterns, and Shelby Harris provides useful, clear, and easily implementable strategies for combating insomnia at all stages of a women's life from her years of clinical experience. Essential reading for any woman trying to understand and overcome her sleep disorder."

—Renee Monderer, M.D., Assistant Professor, Department of Neurology, Montefiore Medical Center

"Most insomnia books do not address the unique biological alterations of sleep throughout a woman's life even though insomnia disproportionately impacts women. In this extraordinary, one-of-a-kind book, Shelby Harris finally talks directly to women about this issue. She is, without a doubt, *the best* sleep psychologist, having helped countless women sleep wonderfully through the night. This book is unimaginably easy to read yet scientifically sound. It summarizes with ease a complex yet essential treatment modality for insomnia, i.e., Cognitive Behavioral Therapy. After reading it, women from any stage of life can conquer their insomnia once and for all!"

—Neomi Shah, M.D., MPH, M.S., Associate Professor of Medicine, Icahn School of Medicine at Mount Sinai, NY, ABIM Board Certified in Sleep Medicine

"With clarity and compassion, Shelby Harris translates complex concepts and counterintuitive approaches into well-defined strategies that will restore sleep health and vitality. Harris offers comfort, support, and guidance to the paralyzing voice that fears the ability to sleep is lost. *The Women's Guide to Overcoming Insomnia* blends years of clinical experience, knowledge of sleep medicine, insightful application, and empathy—creating a trusted companion to any woman in need."

—Rebecca Q. Scott, Ph.D., Diplomate, American Board of Sleep
Medicine, Research Assistant Professor of Neurology,
NYU School of Medicine

"This book is packed full of useful tips and information for every woman who wants to achieve more consolidated, deeper sleep on a regular basis. Whether you have chronic insomnia, an occasional bad night's sleep, or any sleep disruption in between, Shelby Harris will have you sleeping more soundly in no time. This book clearly details the gold standard treatment for insomnia, Cognitive Behavioral Therapy for Insomnia (CBT-I), in an approachable and entertaining way. You will learn to identify factors that trigger and maintain your insomnia, about 'sleep stealers' that negatively impact sleep, and how hormonal cycles affect sleep. Dr. Harris will help you identify and better understand your sleep patterns and then, most importantly, improve them with scientifically-supported interventions. I will recommend this book to all of my patients."

—Rene D. Zweig, Ph.D., Clinical Psychologist, Certified Cognitive Therapist,
and Director of Union Square Cognitive Therapy

"Easy to read, comprehensive, and full of useful information, this book gives helpful advice on practical lifestyle changes and sleep-specific techniques. Often used by sleep specialists, techniques such as sleep restriction therapy, stimulus control, cognitive therapy, and mindfulness can easily be performed by the patient. This is a book that every woman should read to understand good sleep practices, not only those with sleep difficulties."

—Michael Thorpy, M.D., Director, Sleep-Wake Disorders Center, Montefiore
Medical Center, and Professor of Neurology, Albert Einstein College of
Medicine, New York, author of *Encyclopedia of Sleep and Sleep Disorders*

The Women's Guide to Overcoming Insomnia

The Women's Guide to Overcoming Insomnia

Get a Good Night's Sleep
Without Relying on Medication

SHELBY HARRIS, PSY.D.

W. W. Norton & Company
Independent Publishers Since 1923
New York~London

Copyright © 2019 by Shelby Harris

"What if CBT-I Isn't Enough?" copyright © 2019 by Katherine Takayasu

All rights reserved
Printed in the United States of America
First Edition

For information about permission to reproduce selections from this book, write to Permissions, W. W. Norton & Company, Inc., 500 Fifth Avenue, New York, NY 10110

For information about special discounts for bulk purchases, please contact W. W. Norton Special Sales at specialsales@wwnorton.com or 800-233-4830

Manufacturing by Sheridan Books
Book design by Vicki Fischman
Production manager: Katelyn MacKenzie

Library of Congress Cataloging-in-Publication Data

Names: Harris, Shelby, author.
Title: The women's guide to overcoming insomnia : get a good night's sleep without relying on medication / Shelby Harris.
Description: First edition. | New York : W. W. Norton & Company, [2019] | Includes bibliographical references and index.
Identifiers: LCCN 2018050857 | ISBN 9780393711615 (pbk.)
Subjects: LCSH: Insomnia—Alternative treatment—Popular works. | Women—Health and hygiene—Popular works. | Self-care, Health—Popular works.
Classification: LCC RC548 .H36 2019 | DDC 616.8/4982—dc23
LC record available at https://lccn.loc.gov/2018050857

W. W. Norton & Company, Inc., 500 Fifth Avenue, New York, N.Y. 10110
www.wwnorton.com

W. W. Norton & Company Ltd., 15 Carlisle Street, London W1D 3BS

1 2 3 4 5 6 7 8 9 0

To my husband, J: You have been an amazing partner in this crazy journey, and I am eternally grateful to you for your love and support.

To my son, P, and daughter, R: Thank you for being the incredible and inspiring kids that you are. You have given me so much perspective as a therapist and shown me just what is possible in life, even during those tough sleep-deprived months of newborn-hood. Thank you for being awesome sleepers; without your beloved bedtimes and naps, I'm not sure when this book would have gotten finished.

To my parents, M and C: Without your encouragement and love over these years, none of this would be possible.

To my former colleagues at Montefiore Medical Center's Sleep-Wake Disorder Center: I greatly value my longtime experience working with such wonderful sleep physicians and staff; your extensive sleep medicine knowledge base and open collaboration on challenging cases shaped me into the clinician I am today.

Finally, to all my women friends and patients: You've taught me more about life's juggle than you will ever know. I am constantly in awe of how much we take on, and how we frequently come together to support one another in times of need.

CONTENTS

The Women's Guide to Overcoming Insomnia

1.

Why a Book on Sleep Only for Women?

⌒∿⌒

As I sit here at my desk, starting my journey with this book, I'm in a predicament that many women find themselves in at some point in their lifetime: I have a baby at home and am wondering how long it'll take me to write this book and if I'll ever find the time to get it done (update: she's now two and I'm revising/finishing this book). I am struggling with the idea of going back to my clinical work at the hospital and frequently worry about how I will juggle it all. My maternity leave has been equally tough, emotional, and wonderful (and all too brief). I have tried to catch sleep whenever I can, attempted to get my daughter to nap, dealt with hormonal fluctuations and issues with breastfeeding, taken care of household chores, and found time to spend with my husband, older son, and baby.

The stresses are internal and external, physical and mental—physiological changes after just having had a baby, worries I place on myself about getting it all done, a crying hungry baby at 3 a.m.—and they all interfere with sleep. And worst of all, when she does go back to sleep, I'm laying there unable to wind back down and drift off to supreme slumber. These are things that can stress anyone and cause one to lose valuable shut-eye. Even as a psychologist and a sleep expert, I'm not immune to a poor night's sleep now and then. I just know how to prevent it from becoming a regular occurrence at this point in my life.

I'm very much aware that the mental and hormonal firestorm I'm experiencing right now is far too common among women of every age. We're trying to figure out how to get everything on our lists accomplished while also dealing with fluctuating hormones, families, work, and just finding some simple, precious time for ourselves. Poor sleep can occur at any stage in a woman's life, yet the options to most women may appear limited: take sleeping pills, suffer in silence, post on social media at 3 a.m. that you're wide awake with no solution in sight, or power through and say to yourself, "I'll sleep one day," or, worse, "I'll sleep when I'm dead." Although there are times when life gets in the way of sleep, I want you to know that there are effective nonpharmaceutical treatments that help women sleep better on a regular basis.

DIFFERENCES IN SLEEP FOR MEN AND WOMEN

Approximately 11 percent of women have chronic, unremitting insomnia. The 2007 Sleep in America poll by the National Sleep Foundation found that 60 percent of American women get only a few nights of quality sleep per week, and 67 percent have frequent sleep issues. Alarmingly, 43 percent of women reported that daytime sleepiness interferes with their daily activities, including childcare and driving to work. Women often struggle to find an appropriate treatment for their sleep problems and often resort to medication that may compound daytime sleepiness and/or mental fogginess. I am here to help you find a better option.

Insomnia is not gender-blind. Women have a higher risk than men of developing insomnia, at a rate of nearly 3 to 2, and this is observed across most ages from adolescence to menopause (Krishnan & Collop, 2006; Zhang & Wing, 2006). The difference in rates between men and women is even consistent after taking into account any underling psychiatric disorders, such as anxiety or depression. Unlike men, women are susceptible to hormonal and lifestyle changes throughout their lives, which greatly impact the ability to obtain a good night's sleep, and continue with daily activities despite significant fatigue and sleepiness.

For some women, the week before menstruation can be a time of insomnia due to the rise and fall of estrogen and progesterone, with many reporting that sleep improves once the period arrives. Pregnant women have multiple challenges that impact sleep, including hormonal changes, nausea, back pain, discomfort related to constant urination, breast tenderness, a kicking child, a seemingly always growing belly, anxiety, vivid dreams, and increased core body temperature (which can make it tough to fall asleep). Postpartum women have similar issues with hormonal fluctuations, but add to this mix a baby that's up at varying hours of the night, breastfeeding, worry over keeping a human being alive, and loss of any consistent sleep schedule that might have occurred before. And then there's perimenopause, commonly beginning in the late forties, when over a span of approximately 4–5 years (though that can frustratingly vary) a woman's menstrual period spaces out further and further until it ceases. Approximately 50 percent of all women in this stage report sleep difficulties, much higher than the rate of about 31 percent reported by women in their late thirties and early forties (Ciano et al., 2017; Kravitz et al., 2003; Vahratian, 2017). Hormonal fluctuations, hot flashes, sweating, early morning awakenings, minds that won't turn off, and spikes in other sleep disorders such as obstructive sleep apnea can all be factors during this stage of life.

Women typically have very active minds and trouble turning off their to-do lists at night. Even if insomnia isn't an issue, many women feel there's just not enough time to get everything done, and as a result, they don't make time for precious sleep. It feels as if there's just too much to do. The average women gets less than seven hours of sleep per night, despite most women needing more. Women are genetically predisposed to obtain deeper sleep and sleep longer than men, so it is a sad irony that women have a higher rate of insomnia than men and get less sleep than needed.

The National Sleep Foundation poll mentioned above found that, instead of going to bed and making sleep a priority, the vast majority of women either watch TV, finish household chores, spend time on activities with the family, do work, or are on the Internet. Women tend to power through the sleep loss, feeling sluggish and tired without getting the optimal treatment—whether that involves simply making more time for sleep, if insomnia isn't an issue; treating their insomnia, if it is indeed a problem; or getting evaluated for other sleep disorders, such as sleep apnea and restless legs syndrome.

Sleep, health, mood, and quality of life all go hand in hand. Women tend to suffer more than men when it comes to anxiety, worry, and depression. The relationship between sleep and depression and/or anxiety appears to be a two-way street: bad moods cause poor sleep, and poor sleep causes mood disturbances. Poor sleep can increase health risks, especially weight gain. A vicious cycle of sleep loss, leading to bad mood and health problems, leading back to poor sleep is a cycle many women find nearly impossible to break.

Despite the unique challenges that women face related to their sleep (hormonal changes, lifestyle changes, and so on), most books on insomnia lump men and women together. This book is directed specifically at women. It addresses the biological changes that may influence women's sleep patterns over time. Women struggle with so many changes during their lives that impact their bodies and their minds; worrying about "doing it all" on a regular basis usually leaves little time for self-care.

The main focus of this book is treatment for insomnia, while also helping you, the female reader, understand what you can and can't change about your sleep. Just simply picking up this book and thumbing through it is a major first step in acknowledging that you might want to make some changes to your sleep and overall health. Opening up and reading this book, thinking about your insomnia in a thoughtful and almost scientific, detached way will set you on the path toward eventually overcoming the problem. Even if you don't have chronic insomnia, I hope you find this book of use, since it offers simple, straightforward strategies to combat the occasional bad night and help prevent it from becoming a pattern.

Although there are varying ways to treat insomnia—from over-the-counter herbal remedies and pharmacological interventions to nondrug treatments—this book outlines a very effective insomnia treatment called *cognitive behavioral therapy for insomnia* (CBT-I). CBT-I has been extensively studied across many different populations, in both women and men, and has been shown to be a highly effective treatment.

CBT-I is not only a relatively straightforward treatment that is just as effective as taking sleep medications but also yields improvements that persist years after discontinuing active treatment. In fact, the American Academy of Sleep Medicine considers CBT-I the gold standard treatment for insomnia, and most sleep specialists prefer that patients try a solid course of CBT-I before resorting to medication.

I frequently see patients who have been taking sleep aids for years, but once they stop taking medication to help them sleep, the insomnia returns with a vengeance. Instead, CBT-I gives you the tools for proper sleep and helps you retrain both your body and your mind to allow for sleep. Once you complete the active treatment, you will know what to do to continue sleeping well. And while you may experience periods of poor sleep in the future (as do most people), you will have a fully equipped tool belt to manage the insomnia and keep it from becoming a full-fledged problem again.

CBT-I goes far beyond basic sleep hygiene, and this book will teach you how to retrain your body and mind to sleep more efficiently. Treatment sections include education on the many factors that can interfere with sleep, how to develop healthy and effective sleep behaviors, how to get comfortable during pregnancy and perimenopause, skills for calming the mind, individualized sleep/wake scheduling programs, eliminating sleep-incompatible behaviors, ways to challenge your thoughts that might interfere with sleep, and ways to physically unwind before going to bed. Although many of the basics of insomnia treatment are initially the same for both men and women, the treatment sections in this book are crafted to resonate with women while addressing ways to manage situations that are all too common. Factors that may impact your sleep are addressed in detail, with practical strategies to tackle them head-on.

I often see many women in my clinic who suffer needlessly because they have been told—incorrectly—that the only solution to their insomnia is medication. These women suffer because they want to become pregnant, or they have children at home, or they are taking care of aging parents, and they don't want to be "knocked out" throughout the night or feel drugged in the morning. Medical schools generally spend only a few hours training physicians on sleep disorder recognition and treatment (over the entire course of medical education). Understandably, CBT-I is typically something that most physicians are not well versed in, if they even know about it at all (though knowledge about the treatment is becoming more common). It is often easier to find a physician who will prescribe a sleep aid than it is to find a qualified CBT-I provider. But the patient who doesn't want to take medication may be forced to suffer with fatigue day in and day out. The good news is that many people respond to self-help versions of CBT-I, both online and with workbooks, and it is seen as a great first-line intervention for people who have chronic insomnia.

The suggestions provided in this book may yield improvements within just the first few weeks—many patients experience a significant reduction in insomnia symptoms within only five or six weeks of beginning treatment. Keep in mind, though, that for some people the change in sleep can be dramatically fast, but for others it might take weeks or months of gradual changes to your sleep patterns and working on overall consistency with the guidelines discussed here. Many women with insomnia suffer for years on end with poor sleep before getting the help they need. Try to temper your expectations and be patient—you can't force sleep to happen, no matter how hard you try.

And in the event that you're not responding to these suggestions and guidelines as you would like, I asked my fantastic colleague Katie Takayasu, M.D. (a board-certified family medicine physician and integrative medicine specialist) to be a guest author of a chapter discussing other options for insomnia treatment, including pharmaceuticals, supplements, hormonal supplementation, acupuncture, and more. This book also discusses when to see a sleep specialist to make sure nothing else is medically impacting your sleep at night, and how to find a specialist in CBT-I who can take you through the treatment in even greater detail if necessary. What matters most is that you don't suffer from night after night of sleep loss, and ideally this book will help give women some tools to move in the proper direction.

Throughout the book I give examples based on my years of clinical practice working with women who have chronic insomnia. The examples I describe, although derived from actual cases in my practice, are composites—they do not represent actual patients, and they use fictitious names. They nonetheless exemplify patient experiences that I hope you will find enlightening.

PART ONE

Sleep, Insomnia, and Our Hormones

2.

The Nuts and Bolts of Sleep

❧

There's a lot of (mis)information out there about how sleep works. Understanding the basics behind healthy sleep physiology is important because it will lay the groundwork for why many of the behavioral techniques for insomnia are effective. Although these techniques may be difficult to follow through with on a regular basis, knowing *why* you are giving it a fair shot can be extremely helpful, especially at 6:30 a.m. when the last thing you want to do is get out of bed after a tough, sleepless night.

HOW SLEEP WORKS

Two main processes are in effect that help keep you awake, and then put you to sleep as the evening draws near. Keeping both of these mechanisms in check will help you to keep insomnia away.

Sleep Drive, aka "Sleep Hunger"

The concept behind sleep drive is pretty simple: the longer you stay awake, the more pressure you build up in your body to sleep once night arrives (Borbely, 1982). It is an easy idea to grasp if you think of it like hunger. When you wake up, you have essentially just had a full night's "meal" of sleep, so you're not particularly hungry for any sleep. As you stay awake longer and longer throughout the day, the more desire you'll have to sleep. This is just as if you hadn't eaten—you keep your stomach empty hour after hour, and the longer you go, the hungrier and hungrier you get. Once nighttime comes, a healthy sleeper will have accumulated enough sleep drive to be able to easily initiate sleep, thus satiating the sleep appetite.

After a morning when you sleep later than usual, it can sometimes be difficult the next night to fall asleep at the usual time, because you have not been awake long enough to build up a strong enough sleep drive to fall asleep as fast as usual. Naps can be complicated, and as you'll see later in this book, they're typically discouraged with insomnia because they reduce the sleep drive, making it harder to either fall asleep fast at bedtime or stay asleep. Snacking on sleep during the day reduces your appetite for sleep at night.

The Circadian Rhythm and Melatonin

You've likely heard of the circadian rhythm before but might not know much about what it is or why it is important in regulating sleep. We have powerful internal body clocks that affect our behavior and body function. Broken down, *circa* means "about" and *dian* means "a day." The circadian clock works on a roughly 24-hour schedule and produces 24-hour cycles in things like digestion, body temperature, and when you go to sleep and awaken. If I were to have you sit in a room with no windows and no clocks, your body would have a sense that a day has gone by, but it would be just a bit longer—approximately 24.1 hours (which can lead to gradual delays in sleep/wake schedules as time passes if there's no light or time cues). Although the circadian rhythm isn't perfectly set to 24 hours, there are things we innately do to keep our body clocks set, and light and dark exposure are two of the most important biological timekeepers.

The circadian rhythm is responsible for the release of the sleep-promoting hormone melatonin and regulates subtle body temperature fluctuations throughout the day and night. If we record a healthy sleeper's body temperature all day for a few days, we'll see that she has a natural drop in her body temperature approximately 2 hours before bedtime, which then signals the production of melatonin to promote sleepiness. Body temperature will continue to drop very slightly throughout the nighttime hours as melatonin is released. The temperature will be at its lowest at around 3 or 4 a.m., at which time melatonin is then essentially shut off in the brain, helping the body become more alert as the morning comes.

Melatonin is often referred to as the "hormone of darkness" since it needs a dark environment to work at its peak. As daytime gets closer, melatonin production shuts off as light is introduced, thereby helping us wake up and stay awake for the daytime hours. Keeping a consistent light and dark cycle every day is key to helping our circadian rhythm stay on a steady schedule.

The circadian rhythm works to keep us alert throughout the day. There are some normal dips and high points of alertness during the day as well—to be fully wide awake at all hours during the day isn't common. For example, many people feel most alert at midmorning and have a predictable dip in wakefulness at midafternoon. In fact, many cultures have siestas in place to take advantage of the postlunch circadian dip. Once again, though, naps are tricky for people with insomnia (discussed in detail in Chapter 8).

There's also variability in the timing of everyone's circadian rhythm, and it tends to change as we age. Young children typically go to bed early and awaken early, but as they become teenagers their bodies naturally shift to later bed and wake times. As we approach adulthood, the circadian rhythm shifts back a small amount, with many people keeping a roughly 11 p.m. to 7 a.m. sleep/wake schedule (though there's a good deal of variety). Finally, as we become older adults, our circadian rhythms typically move even earlier, signaling us to go to bed and awaken even earlier.

Work schedules, light and dark exposure, meal times, exercise, and other activities work with our body clocks to help keep us on a stable sleep/wake schedule. However, major changes in our sleep/wake schedule can interfere with our ability to sleep. Some people tend to be more affected by abrupt changes in sleep timing, and women with insomnia are typically quite sensitive to them. If, for example, a woman who lives in New York City flies to Los Angeles, she will likely have some trouble with her sleep and daytime fatigue. This occurs because the 3-hour time change places her new desired sleep/wake schedule at odds with her body clock, which is stuck in her old New York City time zone.

Our body clocks thrive on consistency, and it truly takes time for the circadian rhythm to adjust to shifts in lifestyle (such as shifting your sleep schedule 3 hours later on the weekends or traveling across the country). This consistency helps our body know when to stay awake, when to sleep, and when to have the sleep-promoting hormone melatonin released.

How the Sleep Drive and the Circadian Rhythm Work Together to Get Us to Sleep

When we wake in the morning, our sleep drive is rather weak, as we had just been asleep for the night. There's a nice alignment at this time between a weak sleep drive and the start of an alerting signal from the circadian rhythm as melatonin has ceased to be produced. The arrangement between the two processes is often why people tend to feel their most alert in the midmorning hours. As the day goes on and the sleep drive grows stronger, the alerting circadian signal helps keep us awake (albeit with some normal, occasional dips in wakefulness, as mentioned earlier). Once nighttime comes, the two signals come together nicely yet again, with melatonin being released by the circadian rhythm and a hungry sleep drive looking to fall asleep. After a few hours asleep, the sleep drive is satiated rather quickly, but the sleep-promoting part of the circadian rhythm takes over to help keep us asleep for the remainder of the night.

We can easily do many things to throw off the intricate balance between the sleep drive and circadian rhythm. Both drinking caffeine and napping in the afternoon or evening can reduce the sleep drive at night, making it more difficult for the circadian rhythm to start working right away. Once it takes a while to fall asleep, many women may then sleep in the next morning, if they're able to, delaying the circadian rhythm in the morning, therefore making it more difficult to fall asleep the next night.

WHAT HAPPENS WHEN WE SLEEP?

A sleep cycle occurs when we fall asleep and then cycle through various stages of sleep, from non-REM sleep (which includes both lighter sleep and restorative deep sleep) to more active, memory- and emotion-consolidating REM sleep (when we most typically dream). After each sleep cycle, which typically lasts about 90 minutes, we have a brief awakening and then go right back to sleep, repeating the sleep cycle again. There is some variability from person to person in the length of the sleep cycle, which often depends on age, medical/psychiatric history, and medications. A healthy young woman sleeper may go through five to seven sleep cycles a night, with a brief awakening after each one. The awakening is so fast that there's little to no recollection of them when morning arrives.

Many women with insomnia often report that they desire to sleep through the entire night without any awakenings at all. This is typically unrealistic, especially as we age. To have a more tempered view of what sleep should look like at your stage in life will help set up realistic expectations.

Women have been shown to have more slow-wave, deep stage 3

sleep than do men. This gender difference has been documented as early as 6 months of age. Slow-wave sleep is the most refreshing and deepest part of sleep that most people hope to obtain every night. Men's nightly percentage of deep sleep begins to decline in their twenties, yet women will hold on until their thirties, with younger women waking up less frequently than men. Women's circadian systems also tend to hold onto their patterns longer and are more resistant than men's to changes due to age.

If you're a woman reading this book, you're probably now asking yourself, *If I have this gender advantage for deep sleep, why am I, and so many other women, suffering from insomnia?* Good question.

The answer to this lies in our hormones. Women may be able to get deeper sleep, but we aren't able to get a lot of it. Total sleep time becomes shorter and more disrupted. These hormonal changes are discussed in more depth in Chapter 4, but for now, suffice it to say that hormonal changes during the menopause transition can cause women to awaken more frequently. Issues such as having to urinate more at night, as well a chronic pain from a variety of issues, such as arthritis or neuropathy, can all lead to broken sleep. Because sleep becomes more broken as we age, a decrease in the *quality* of sleep is most commonly noted, along with greater fatigue during the daytime hours. As a result of these changes, it is likely unrealistic that a woman in her fifties will sleep as she did as a younger adult. But although these changes set the stage for the development of sleep problems, they are not a guarantee!

WHY DO WE NEED TO SLEEP?

Sleep is extremely important, yet we still do not have a solid answer regarding exactly *why* we sleep. Quality sleep is vital for our mental and physical health, overall quality of life, and safety. While we're sleeping, our brains are preparing us for the next day by forming new connections and pathways to learn new information and consolidate what we have learned previously. Sleep is important for tissue growth, as well as repairing heart and blood vessels. We know a lot from studies on sleep deprivation: poor sleep results in worsened immune function, cognitive problems (such as trouble with memory, attention), coordination issues, cardiovascular complications, and worsened mood. In essence, every disease in modern society (diabetes, cognition, cardiovascular disease, suicide, etc.) has strong links to insufficient sleep. Quality sleep regulates our immune system and has even been shown to flush from the brain toxic proteins that have been linked to dementia.

EXERCISE, DIET, AND . . . SLEEP

Sure, a proper diet and moderate exercise are important factors in overall physical health, but did you know that obtaining regular, quality sleep is just as important? Obtaining adequate sleep on a regular basis is the foundation on which exercise and diet work best. Sleep deprivation influences two key hormones in our body: leptin and ghrelin. Leptin is the hormone that tells our body to stop eating, giving us the sensation that we are full. Ghrelin, on the other hand, is a hormone that gives us a hunger signal and tells us to eat. When we don't get enough sleep, the leptin/ghrelin balance is shifted, with a drop in leptin and an increase in ghrelin. As a result, the signal that tells us we're full becomes weaker, and the signal that tells us to eat is strengthened.

Researchers at the University of Chicago in 2010 followed ten overweight adults for two 2-week intervals (Nedeltcheva, Kilkus, Imperial, Schoeller & Penev, 2010). In the first 2-week interval, participants were observed in the laboratory and encouraged to obtain 8.5 hours of sleep each night. They were all placed on a balanced diet with very mild calorie restriction. Daytime hours were spent doing activities similar to what the participants usually did at home. In the second 2-week interval, participants were kept on the same diet but were limited to 5.5 hours of sleep each night. Although the groups lost the same amount of weight overall, the well-rested group lost dramatically more fat (which is ideal), whereas the sleep-deprived group lost more muscle mass (which is not ideal).

There's also some research suggesting that variability in the timing of our sleep schedule may contribute to a thicker waistline. A 2013 study at Brigham Young University followed more than 300 college-age women for a few weeks, assessing them for body fat composition and keeping track of their sleep patterns for 1 week (Bailey et al., 2013). Results showed that participants who obtained less than 6.5 or more than 8.5 hours of sleep per night had higher body fat percentages.

What is novel in this study is that the researchers looked at the timing of sleep and its impact on body fat composition. They found that a consistent bedtime and, more important, a consistent wake time were related to lower body fat. Participants who had more than 90 minutes of variation in their sleep/wake times were more likely to have higher body fat composition than those with less than 60 minutes of variation.

Not sleeping in allows for us to be out of bed and active for more hours, which helps with lowering body fat. The researchers also noted that sleep quality greatly impacted body composition. Participants who slept better had less body fat. When your sleep is disrupted, the benefits from that rest period are diminished.

Another key benefit to improving your sleep is that it will likely give you more energy. With that comes more ability to exercise and get the most out of your workouts. We know that combining diet and exercise is a key to weight loss and healthy living, but if you add a full night of sleep to the equation, you'll reap the benefits even more.

THE GOOD AND BAD OF SLEEP LOSS

In some ways, sleep loss may have a positive effect on the following night's sleep. In fact, the sleep drive grows stronger the longer we are awake before trying to go to sleep. It is important to remain awake through each day in order to build up enough sleep drive to produce a full night's sleep.

Extended periods of sleep loss, of course, may have some bad effects as well. People who are totally deprived of sleep usually become very sleepy, have trouble concentrating, and are irritable. However, they can continue most normal daytime activities even without any sleep at all the night before. When allowed to sleep after a longer than normal period of being awake, most of us will tend to sleep longer and deeper than we usually do. Although we may not recover all of the sleep time we lost, we do usually recover the deep sleep we lost during longer than usual periods without sleep. Hence, our body's sleep drive has some ability to make up for times when we don't get the amount of sleep we need. This is an important concept to grasp since it will come into play in later in this book.

Takeaway Message: How Sleep Works

- ✓ Sleep is important to many aspects of our daily life, yet many women with insomnia continue to push on day after day.
- ✓ Two major processes regulate our sleep: the circadian rhythm and the sleep drive.
- ✓ The circadian rhythm helps keep our clock body in tune overall (sleeping at night and awake during the day). The sleep drive is like an appetite for sleep, building up throughout the day and relieved at night.
- ✓ The longer we are awake during the day, the greater the sleep drive at night, and it is even stronger when it is timed properly with our circadian rhythm for sleep.

3.

What Is Insomnia?

It is totally normal to have trouble with sleep now and again. Nearly 50 percent of the population has had an occasional bout of poor sleep. I'm always skeptical of the few people who tell me they have *never* had a poor night of sleep in their entire life—during stressful (good or bad) events, before a job interview, or a before a big test. Anxiety and stress are meant to light a fire under us to act on the problem at hand—there's an evolutionary purpose to this. Think about it: we're built to sleep in caves, and from time to time there might be a lion outside threatening our young sleeping beside us. If we choose to be in a deep slumber that entire night, it is highly likely that the lion is going to win out. Transfer that analogy to today's times, except the next day there's twenty things on the to-do list for the kids and a work presentation that isn't completely finished for the morning. Our body reacts to these stressors the exact same way as if it were a lion outside the cave: lighter sleep and trouble turning off the brain that's trying to tackle the problems at hand.

If you think your sleep issues are persistent and are regularly impacting your ability to go through your daily life, it might be time to intervene. So yes, while it is totally normal to have an occasional subpar night's sleep, it is not normal to suffer from poor sleep on a regular basis. For example, if you're promoted to a new job at work and then after a few weeks into the new position you continue having trouble getting a good night's sleep, you might want to start thinking about getting treatment for your insomnia before it gets any worse.

There is some *mild* variation with our sleep from night to night, and on top of that, not every single night of every week is going to be perfect. This is normal, and you should work to internalize this. Even if you are successfully treating for your insomnia, it is unrealistic to think you'll never have a poor night or stretch of sleep now and then.

So how do you know if you've crossed from the "occasional night of poor sleep" over into an actual insomnia disorder? Even though the sporadic bout of insomnia is common, chronic severe insomnia is not uncommon, with approximately 10 percent of U.S. adults suffering from the problem (National Institutes of Health, 2005). According to the fifth edition of the *Diagnostic and Statistical Manual of Mental Disorders* (American Psychiatric Association, 2013), insomnia disorder occurs when you have trouble falling asleep, staying asleep, or awakening too early for *at least* 3 nights a week for *at least* 3 months. Acute (short-term) insomnia is diagnosed after just 1 month, but chronic (long-term) insomnia has to go on for at least 3 months. In addition to this, it has to create a problem for you or someone in your life, which might include frustration laying in bed awake at night, daytime fatigue or excessive sleepiness, being late to school/work, irritability, anxiety as night draws near, worsening of depression/anxiety/stress/pain/medical issues as a result of poor sleep, mental fatigue, memory problems—the list is endless.

Despite all this, I do not necessarily believe that you must wait a whole 3 months to qualify for chronic insomnia before you start sleep treatment—that is completely unnecessary. A lot of the strategies in this book can be used even during one night of poor sleep. Some others, however, such as sleep restriction, require 1–2 weeks of sleep diaries to properly engage in the technique.

You might not have chronic, unremitting insomnia, but if you have an occasional bad night, the suggestions in this book are of use to everyone who has an occasional bad night. While it is unrealistic to expect a full night of perfect sleep every single night of your life, why not see if there's a way to improve upon what you may already be doing? It might gain you some extra shut-eye.

An overall goal is to attempt to get a solid night of sleep most nights of the week. In the sleep field, we use the term *sleep efficiency percentage* (discussed in Chapter 10 on how to consolidate your sleep). In short, sleep efficiency percentage describes what percentage of your time in bed you're actually asleep. Our goal is to spend at least 85 percent of the time in bed asleep (and ideally 90 percent). This suggests that some time is spent awake while falling asleep, maybe a brief awakening or two at night, and possibly waking up just before your wake time—it is normal to have a small amount of time in bed awake, but a more consolidated night is the goal. The other thing to keep in mind is that we want to aim for 85–90 percent *on average* for the week, taking into account a few nights each week when sleep is suboptimal . . . which is totally normal.

HOW DOES INSOMNIA DEVELOP?

Older schools of thought typically believed that insomnia was simply a symptom of something else that caused the sleep issue. As a result, doctors would often be on the search for "primary" issues that were the root of the insomnia, whether they were medical or psychiatric. For example, if you suffered from both depression and insomnia, the prevailing theory for quite some time was that depression was the primary issue and the insomnia was a secondary one and that treating the depression would resolve the insomnia. Another example I commonly see in my practice is patients with chronic pain who also suffer from sleep issues. This leads to a constant search for pain relief in the hope that sleep will improve as well.

Although a lot of doctors still believe in this primary/secondary theory, it is actually quite outdated. Dr. Arthur Spielman broke through the more standard way of thinking about insomnia with his "3P" model of insomnia, with the three Ps representing *predisposing* factors, *precipitating* factors, and *perpetuating* factors. I describe each of these in the sections that follow.

Spielman's theory is a simple yet elegant way to explain the development of insomnia in many patients, and I find that it resonates with a lot of the women I work with. Having a good understanding of what leads to insomnia is extremely important because it helps lay the basis for the treatment strategies proposed in this book. There is a significant amount of research supporting it, and, as I hope you'll see shortly, it makes a strong case against the typical primary/secondary theory of insomnia.

Predisposing Factors

Among Spielman's three main factors that all play together to create an episode of insomnia, predisposing factors are the bedrock. These are things that might make you susceptible to developing insomnia, but their mere existence doesn't necessarily mean you will definitely develop insomnia. For example, just because your parents both had insomnia doesn't guarantee you'll have it, but it does increase your chances since there is a genetic component to insomnia, especially if your mom had the problem as well.

When trying to pinpoint any predisposing factors, I often find it helpful to break them down into "bio-psycho-social" elements. Biological ("bio") factors involve your own medical history (or family medical history), which may make you more likely to have an episode (or more) of poor sleep. This can include things like cancer, fibromyalgia, and menstrual changes such as perimenopause. As mentioned above, women are more likely than men to develop insomnia, so your gender alone leads to an increased risk of developing insomnia. I also often hear patients say things like, "I was a light sleeper all of my life, but it was never an issue until now," or "My mind has always been very active at night, but now I just can't seem to turn it off."

Psychological ("psych") factors are exactly as they sound. Maybe you're a "type A" personality and have a lot of stress and difficulty letting things be less than perfect. Poor sleep might develop in the presence of depression, anxiety, bipolar disorder, trauma, stress, and tension, though it doesn't always have to be this way.

Social factors are a bit trickier for many people to identify. They usually include some external elements that may have been present for a while but haven't influenced your sleep, and then another event really kicks insomnia off. This could include having children in the house who don't sleep well themselves, working varying shifts, having a spouse who is a poor/noisy/restless sleeper, financial or job insecurity, or having a bed partner (husband, wife, significant other, etc.) who keeps a different sleep schedule (such as with shift work). Like I said earlier, these bio-psycho-social elements are ones that merely set the stage for developing insomnia; they don't mean you'll definitely develop insomnia.

Now, see if you can figure out what your predisposing factor(s) might be that contribute to your insomnia (now or in the past). Use Form 3.1 at the end of this chapter to help you think about and recognize which predisposing factors you have in your history.

Precipitating Factors

Precipitating factors are specific events that actually set off an episode of insomnia, whether short term or chronic. Once again, I find it is easiest to break these factors down into bio-psycho-social stressors to try to pinpoint when the insomnia began.

Biological stressors may include medical problems (such as a new medical diagnosis or recurrence of an old one, starting treatment for cancer, or starting steroids for chronic pain and fibromyalgia), the start of perimenopause with hot flashes and night sweats, or discomfort from pregnancy or childbirth. Psychological precipitants might be an onset of depression, anxiety, a traumatic event, or significant stress at work or home. Social factors could include financial problems, work issues, a child who is having trouble at school or in social settings, or marriage problems. Social precipitants may also include having a newborn and being hypervigilant for awakenings/feedings, staying up worrying about an adolescent who is out late (and then not being able to fall back to sleep once your child is finally home!), or caregiving for an older parent in the house. Remember, good stress is stress as well. People often have disrupted sleep around times of getting married, starting new jobs, going to college, and so on.

Yes, the waters get a bit muddied among the bio-psycho-social issues here (for example, losing a job could cause significant financial stress for someone, as well as depression—a recipe for insomnia). Don't get bogged down with where the line falls exactly; this framework helps you think of all the issues that might play into the development of your insomnia.

Some women can pinpoint the exact reason/time when their insomnia began, whereas others struggle significantly with locating any reason whatsoever. These women frequently say, "I've had insomnia for so long, I just don't know when it started or why," or "It started in June 2012, but I have no idea what started the issue." Although having a good understanding of what may have contributed to the insomnia episode is helpful, it isn't 100 percent crucial in treatment. I've seen plenty of patients who couldn't figure out an exact cause for their insomnia, yet they were still able to seek successful treatment.

Now, see if you can figure out what your precipitating factor(s) might be that triggered to your insomnia (now or in the past). Use Form 3.1 at the end of this chapter to help you think about and recognize which factors you experienced.

Perpetuating Factors

To review, we start with the bedrock: the predisposing factors. These are the things that are built into you or are in your life/lifestyle that don't necessarily change from day to day or cause insomnia. They set the stage but don't always mean you'll get it. Then, a precipitating event happens, which leads you to an episode of insomnia. Now you're not sleeping . . . a few nights go by, and little sleep. More nights go by, and still not great. A few weeks go by, and now the nights turn into a month or more of poor sleep. After a month or two of multiple nights of poor sleep week after week, most people with insomnia tend to do whatever they can to either get more sleep or cope with getting through the day however possible. That's where perpetuating factors come into play.

I consider insomnia to be a disorder that's a result of common sense. This may sound strange, but common sense is typically what's getting many people in trouble when it comes to their sleep. Let's take Lucy, for example, a married 45-year-old stay-at-home mother of three. Lucy started noticing some symptoms consistent with perimenopause, including early morning awakenings, occasional hot flashes, irregular periods, breast tenderness, and fatigue. She consulted her gynecologist, who agreed that perimenopause was likely beginning, and Lucy decided to "ride it out." However, after 8 months of poor sleep, mental fog, and irritability, she ended up in my office telling me that she was "desperate" to sleep as she struggled with juggling the needs of her three children during the day.

When I asked Lucy about her typical sleep/wake schedule, there wasn't one anymore (before her insomnia she'd kept a 10:30 p.m.–6 a.m. sleep schedule). Around 2 weeks after her insomnia began, she started to go to bed whenever she could after all of her children were in bed, in the hope that "tonight will be the night I'll get more sleep." She would get in bed when tired, but not particularly sleepy, and then lay in bed watching TV for a few hours to quiet her brain, only to fall asleep 3 hours later with the TV on in the background. She would then wake up 2 hours later, turn off the TV, and take another hour to fall back asleep (usually just laying still in bed in the hope that she'd fall asleep). On occasion, when desperate after a really rough night before, she would take either a prescribed or over-the-counter sleep aid or use alcohol to sedate herself. During the week, once her kids were up she would get up, since she had no other options as her husband left early for work. On the weekends, she would lay in bed for 2 extra hours, hoping to catch up on her sleep. During the daytime, she would try (rarely successfully) to take a nap in her car when waiting for her children at the bus stop, and she was well known at her local coffee shop—she was there two or three times a day for a latte to give her some extra energy.

Lucy is a nice example of someone who fell into the trap of common sense, where perpetuating behaviors began to take hold once insomnia started. She was so tired and run down every day that she placed a lot of mental emphasis on obtaining sleep and started doing things she normally didn't in order to sleep. Examples include sleep extension (going to bed early or staying in bed late hoping to catch extra sleep), napping, using more caffeine, staying in bed trying to force sleep to happen, and worrying more about sleep as the night comes in the hope that increased thinking about it will help sleep happen. Other common perpetuating behaviors include clock watching throughout the night, calling out from work or going to work late, using medications or alcohol for sleep, and avoiding morning and evening activities for fear of being fatigued.

All of these are common sense commandments that the brain is telling someone with insomnia. Tired? Go to bed early! Sleep in! Nap! Have some (lots of?!) coffee! The problem here, though, is that solid research shows that, even though there may have been precipitating events that kicked off the episode of insomnia, in a vast majority of situations it is these perpetuating, commonsense behaviors that actually maintain the insomnia.

This is precisely why changing some of the old sleep habits using CBT-I can be a challenge for many—you're truly going *against* your common sense to initiate evidence-based treatment strategies. In all honestly, this common sense is so strong that I even find myself falling for it and have to catch myself from time to time. I'm not immune to a stretch of poor sleep now and then, and my desire to sleep in, lay in bed trying to force sleep to happen, and rest/take naps during the day is extremely powerful—until I remind myself that it is the totally opposite thing I need to do if I want to keep insomnia away.

Now, see if you can figure out what commonsense responses you've had to your insomnia—your perpetuating factor(s). Use Form 3.1 at the end of this chapter to help you think about and recognize which factors may be contributing to your ongoing insomnia.

INSOMNIA CO-OCCURRING WITH MEDICAL AND PSYCHIATRIC DISORDERS

The 3P model of insomnia development has greatly influenced the way sleep specialists think about the causes of insomnia and how we should approach the problem. When a medical or psychiatric condition exists along with insomnia, it does not necessarily mean that the two are immediately linked or (even if they *are* linked) that they're significantly influencing each other. Therefore, we sleep specialists now refer to the association as *co-occurring*, or existing alongside, rather than *secondary*, which implies one condition causes the other. For example, someone might have insomnia and depression, but that does not necessarily mean the depression 100 percent caused the insomnia. I find that it is sometimes a chicken-and-egg situation: did the insomnia lead to your anxiety, or did the anxiety lead to your insomnia? Even if the depression did lead to more time in bed avoiding things and ruminating (thereby fueling the beginning of the insomnia), it is still advisable to address the insomnia as a separate issue in a comprehensive treatment plan.

Moreover, if we use the old-school approach of treating only the "underlying" diagnosis, often the insomnia doesn't resolve since we aren't addressing it directly. So, as discussed earlier in this chapter, the older approach to insomnia was to treat the predisposing and precipitating factors that presumably started the insomnia, such as depression, anxiety, pain, cancer, or perimenopause, since it was believed that treating those factors would then resolve the insomnia. But, as I hope is now abundantly clear, it is the development of the perpetuating, commonsense factors that really makes the insomnia take on a life—and diagnosis—of its own that warrants its own separate, targeted treatment. No more primary and secondary ideas; instead, "X" plus insomnia co-occur, and treatment is aimed at both issues in the vast majority of people.

Takeaway Message: How Insomnia Develops

✓ Think about how your insomnia may have developed using the 3P model (review your answers on Form 3.1 to help you with this).
✓ Review the perpetuating behaviors you identified on Form 3.1—the ones you developed in the face of developing insomnia. These are the factors that you will want to focus on with the strategies in this book.

FORM 3.1: **Using the 3P Model to Examine
How Your Insomnia Developed**

Check all that apply.

Predisposing Factors: *Things you had from the start*

- ☐ Family members with sleep or psychiatric disorders
- ☐ Prior history of being a poor sleeper
- ☐ Chronic pain
- ☐ Light sleeper
- ☐ Sensitivity to hormonal changes
- ☐ A busy, active brain, especially at night but also can be during the day
- ☐ Anxiety, worry, rumination
- ☐ Depression or bipolar disorder
- ☐ History of trauma
- ☐ Being a "type A" person
- ☐ Shift work
- ☐ Having a spouse that works shifts
- ☐ Other factors: _____

Precipitating Factors: *What may have started this insomnia episode*

- ☐ Medical problems (new or recurring diagnosis, fibromyalgia, surgery, allergies, cancer, diabetes, etc.)
- ☐ New medication, stopping a medication
- ☐ Work stress, job insecurity
- ☐ Death in family/friend circle
- ☐ Onset of a psychiatric disorder
- ☐ Perimenopause
- ☐ Childbirth
- ☐ Having a child, partner, or family member who doesn't sleep well
- ☐ Moving
- ☐ Divorce, breaking off a relationship
- ☐ Financial insecurity
- ☐ Changing work shifts, bed partner changing work shifts
- ☐ Getting married
- ☐ New job or new position at work
- ☐ Other factors: _____

Perpetuating Factors: What you did (and may still do) to cope with poor sleep

- [ ] Nap
- [ ] Go to bed early in hope of falling asleep
- [ ] Lay in bed later in morning or attempt to sleep later in hope of catching up on sleep
- [ ] Attempt to sleep in later on the weekends to "catch up" on lost sleep from the week
- [ ] Spend more time in bed at night (or during the day)
- [ ] Drink caffeine/take stimulants to cope with fatigue
- [ ] Use electronics at night when unable to sleep
- [ ] Dread the nighttime as it comes closer
- [ ] Watch the clock at night
- [ ] Use the snooze alarm or turn off/avoid alarm clock altogether
- [ ] Take over-the-counter or prescribed sleep medications
- [ ] Drink alcohol to help you sleep
- [ ] Avoid or cancel any activities that might be perceived as difficult after a poor night's sleep (such as exercise, work meetings, house chores, driving)
- [ ] Avoid nighttime activities out of fear they will be too stimulating or you won't have energy to do them
- [ ] Tell people you haven't slept well as a subtle sign for them not to expect too much from you
- [ ] Other factors: _____

4.

As Your Hormones Change, So Will Your Sleep

There are over fifty hormones in the female body, with each providing a specific biological function. The two primary female hormones, estrogen and progesterone, are delicately balanced throughout the menstrual cycle, and shifts in their levels over time impact our ability to sleep well. Estrogen is produced in a woman's eggs, fatty tissue, and adrenal glands and is the main female sex hormone tied to the monthly menstruation cycle. Estrogen is also a key player in maintaining a healthy weight, heart health, and bone strength and bolstering mood and cognition. Of particular relevance here, estrogen also helps women fall asleep and stay asleep.

Progesterone is estrogen's relative. Produced in a woman's eggs, adrenal glands, and placenta (during a pregnancy), it is extremely important in maintaining a healthy pregnancy. It is also very important in regulating mood and bone strength. It is known to be sedating and relaxing as it enhances production of GABA, the brain's calming neurotransmitter. Low levels of progesterone have been linked with broken sleep, early morning awakenings, and anxiety in many women.

THE MENSTRUAL CYCLE, HORMONES, AND SLEEP

When comparing younger boys and girls, the rates of insomnia are even until early teenage years, when girls hit puberty and begin menstruation. At this point, girls show a clear dominance in sleep disturbance, likely due in part to hormonal shifts, though there may be other societal factors at play as well.

The menstrual cycle follows three distinct phases that then repeat roughly every month. Day 1 of a woman's period is the start of the *menstrual phase*. This is when estrogen and progesterone are both low, and some women report more difficulty with insomnia at the beginning of this phase. After menstruation, a woman then moves into the *follicular phase*, when estrogen and progesterone levels begin to rise in preparation for the body to release another egg. These elevated hormones can cause some women to feel drowsy. After the egg is released, the body is now preparing for possible fertilization and pregnancy by having peak estrogen and progesterone levels, typically 1 week before menstruation. Due to these high hormonal levels, especially progesterone, many women feel that sleep is easiest during this phase. If the egg is then unfertilized—as it typically is most of the time—a sharp decline in hormones (especially progesterone) happens and the uterus then sheds the lining, starting the menstrual cycle all over again.

Many women note that the three or so days leading up to and beginning menstruation are quite troublesome for sleep and mood. This is typically due to the sharp decrease in progesterone, but once it begins to rise again after menstruation, sleep and mood level off. This drop in progesterone and estrogen at the start of menstruation is linked with headaches, anxiety, low mood, and severe cramps. Not surprisingly, all of these symptoms can impact the ability to sleep well. When I work with women in their twenties and thirties in my office, once they begin tracking their sleep we frequently note an increase in sleep problems in sleep diaries and link it up with their menstrual cycle.

Younger women report stress surrounding defining their identity as a woman, whether at work, in a relationship, or socially. Sleep isn't always a priority, and when they want to sleep, it is difficult to obtain if their mind is unable to turn off and their bodies have not sufficiently wound down.

PREGNANCY AND SLEEP

Fluctuating hormonal levels throughout pregnancy frequently lead to disrupted sleep through much of this time, with the second trimester usually the best time for ideal slumber. Physical discomfort, stress of a major life change on the horizon, and hormonal changes all work in concert to impact sleep.

During the first trimester, sleep changes are quite evident during both the day and night. Progesterone is heightened during this time to protect the pregnancy, and given its relaxing properties, women frequently report being extremely sleepy during the daytime. These hormonal changes cause the common symptoms of nausea and vomiting, frequent urination day and night, and back pain—all reasons for broken and shallower nighttime sleep. The urge to nap is quite strong during the first trimester. Although sleep may be interrupted, women in the first trimester are noted to sleep more than usual in a 24-hour time span. A newly pregnant mother's body is working in overdrive to nurture the baby as the placenta (the organ that feeds the baby until birth) is forming and requires more energy from the body.

As mentioned earlier, the second trimester tends to be slightly better, as nausea and vomiting typically resolve at this time for most women. However, more physical discomforts begin to take hold, including lower back pain, heartburn, and leg cramping. Nighttime urination is often less of a problem at this stage because the growing fetus moves above the bladder and places less pressure on it.

The third trimester is the most stressful for most pregnant women.

Typical physical discomfort includes sinus congestion, back pain, constipation, shortness of breath, heartburn, leg cramps, and frequent nighttime urination due to the baby putting pressure on the bladder. Stress, excitement, and anxiety are also a big part of this phase of pregnancy, leading many pregnant women to have extremely vivid dreams as well. Evolutionary theorists believe that the pregnant mom's sleep becomes more broken at this time as a way to prepare for the disrupted sleep that is about to happen once baby arrives. It would be so nice to get deep, restful slumber in the months before having a baby, but I do understand where this evolutionary adaptation comes from: easing soon-to-be parents into the harsh reality of broken sleep with a newborn who has no set sleep cycle.

In addition to the usual insomnia that occurs during pregnancy for the vast majority of women, the risk of developing a few other sleep disorders at this stage is also higher and should be evaluated if necessary. Snoring, sleep apnea, restless legs syndrome, and periodic limb movement disorder can each impact the pregnancy and the mom's health (these sleep disorders are discussed in greater detail in Chapter 5).

POSTPARTUM: THE START OF "MOMSOMNIA"

The time shortly after childbirth is filled with a tornado of emotions, highs and lows, and utter exhaustion. The type of delivery (vaginal or caesarean), number of babies birthed, and breastfeeding (and any complications associated with it) are just a few of the things that can disrupt sleep. Newborns are born without a set sleep/wake cycle—they have not been exposed to enough light and dark in utero to develop a predictable circadian rhythm. In addition, they need seemingly constant feedings to develop and grow as they should. New moms are often under a great deal of stress trying to make it all work, juggling everything themselves, and are not always that great at asking for help. They are also genetically programmed to keep one ear open at all times for the baby, making it hard to get a restful, deep sleep even when sleep is finally obtained by both mom and baby. "Sleep when the baby sleeps"—yes, but it isn't always so easy. I always struggled with that recommendation myself. And if there are other children at home as well, things are just even more hectic all around. Stress, hormones, and Mother Nature all work together to make sleep difficult at the very beginning.

As the baby develops a sleep/wake rhythm and does not require constant feedings every two or three hours at night, infant nighttime sleep lengthens. By 4–8 months, most babies begin sleeping through the night. While mom might finally be able to sleep longer stretches at night, many women report rarely being able to obtain deep sleep—likely due to keeping an ear/eye out "just in case" anything happens with the baby at night. In essence, they're asleep, but there's a tiny part of the brain keeping watch at all times. Far too often, I see women in my practice who immediately pinpoint the start of their insomnia as when they had their babies.

Women in this stage are often stressed with juggling everything: taking care of the children and their significant others, making sure that dinner is on the table, homework is completed, dishes are in the wash, and there are enough clean clothes. There are too many balls in the air for most women to juggle effortlessly; throw a full time job on top of it—and the possibility of doing it solo, as so many women have to contend with—and the balls can feel as if they'll drop at any time.

SLEEP DURING PERIMENOPAUSE

Many people think of menopause as the time when one's menstruation begins to taper off, but in actuality, it is defined as the cessation of menses altogether for a time span of one year. The transition phase (formally known as *perimenopause*) from the reproductive stage of life to menopause typically takes around 4–6 years, though it can be longer— even upward of 10 years. The median age of onset for perimenopause is

47 years old and the final period is around 51 years old. The menstrual cycle is lengthened by at least 7 days in early perimenopause; however, toward the end of perimenopause, the time between cycles can lengthen to be over 60 days.

During perimenopause, a woman's hormone levels may swing back and forth intensely, leading to many of the bothersome symptoms that she experiences during this stage of life. Hot flashes, night sweats, and awakening with an overactive brain are extremely common during this time and greatly impact sleep for many women. Hot flashes are particularly problematic for those who suffer from them, and they typically begin later in perimenopause and peak within the first 2 years after the final menstrual period. Over the next few years they slowly decline—rarely do they hang around permanently (though it might feel as if you'll be suffering forever during a particularly bad spell of them).

While many women decide to "ride it out" during perimenopause, or try other medication treatments and/or CBT-I, others find that nothing has worked and are understandably extremely frustrated and tired. A detailed talk with a knowledgeable gynecologist regarding the risks and benefits of various hormone replacement therapies may be warranted (see Chapter 14 more discussion on this topic).

In this phase of life, women typically report stress related to redefining their identity. For example, some women who were stay-at-home moms may begin to face empty nest syndrome as her children leave the house and go to college. Other women are growing older and chose to have children at a later stage in life (something that is much more common now) and are dealing instead with active adolescent issues despite the desire to have some down time for themselves for once. Caring for aging parents, careers intensifying or even changing at this point, and stressors at home often fuel marital problems and divorce. Health problems start happening more often, particularly chronic pain issues, sleep apnea, diabetes, heart disease, and restless legs syndrome.

SLEEP DURING POSTMENOPAUSE

Once a woman has not menstruated for 12 months, she is considered to be postmenopause. At this stage of life, progesterone is no longer produced (remember, it was highly linked to supporting a healthy pregnancy). Estrogen is still produced in lower levels but does not dramatically fluctuate as it once did. Most women note a softening of the distressing perimenopausal symptoms that impacted quality of life, mood, and sleep, although this can vary greatly. Anxiety, low mood, fatigue, disrupted sleep, hot flashes, and night sweats tend to ease with the steadier hormonal levels, and many women breathe a sigh of relief once again. Rates of sleep apnea drastically increase at this point, and any concerning sleepiness should be evaluated by a sleep medicine professional.

Retirement also frequently happens at this time in life for many women. While it may bring about less stress and better sleep, given the fewer overall life demands, some older adults note significant worsening of sleep at this point in life, given the loosening of overall routine and sleep schedules. I frequently see older adults who note that retirement was actually the start of their sleep problems, citing financial stressors, lack of structure, potential moves to assisted living, and nocturnal urination as contributing factors.

Postmenopausal women also report more issues with pain and other medical disorders than their younger counterparts. Along with this come more medications as well, all things that can disrupt sleep. Certain heart medications, blood pressure medications, decongestants, antidepressants, and pain medications can impact sleep at night and sometimes make one excessively sleepy during the daytime.

POLYCYSTIC OVARIAN SYNDROME

Polycystic ovarian syndrome (PCOS) is a hormonal disorder that is very common in women, but it manifests in a wide variety of symptoms (metabolic, reproductive, and mental health), making it difficult for clinicians to recognize and diagnose appropriately. Symptoms typically first appear around puberty, and girls and women with PCOS often note excessive body hair and severe acne (especially on the face, neck, chest, and back) and are frequently overweight or obese. They often have higher androgen (a male hormone) levels and infrequent periods.

PCOS is usually diagnosed with a standard gynecological pelvic exam, blood tests to measure hormonal and glucose tolerance levels, and an ultrasound. On ultrasound, the ovaries may be noted to have numerous small cysts (sacks of fluid) and not release eggs for ovulation on a predictable basis. As a result, many women with PCOS find it challenging— though not impossible—to become pregnant.

Although no exact cause is yet known for PCOS, many agree that insulin resistance is a key player. During this process, insulin levels rise in the body as more and more insulin is produced. This excess insulin leads to more androgen production, which in turn leads to ovulation difficulties.

Chronic insomnia, especially trouble falling asleep and staying asleep, is common in women with PCOS, as well as obstructive sleep apnea and higher rates of anxiety and depression. It has also been linked to gestational diabetes, type 2 diabetes, uterine cancer, high cholesterol, and high blood pressure. Although it is commonly thought that sleep apnea occurs because many women with PCOS are overweight or obese, this is being challenged as research begins to take hold in this field. Higher rates of insomnia and obstructive sleep apnea are seen in normal-weight women with PCOS, and researchers such as Fernandez et al. (2018) even suggest that poor sleep may play a role in causing or worsening of PCOS symptoms, instead of always resulting from the hormonal imbalance.

Diagnosing PCOS early is extremely helpful, as it is often a lifelong management process. A thoughtful discussion with a gynecologist is extremely helpful in these cases, as it can bring predictability and sense of normalcy to the lives of women who suffer from this disorder. Many women with PCOS take specific combination estrogen-progestin birth control pills to regulate their hormonal imbalance and allow their menstrual cycle to become more predictable. Other medications (such as clomiphene, letrozole, or metformin) are available to help increase ovulation and improve the chances of becoming pregnant.

Women with PCOS are encouraged to maintain a healthy weight overall, though this can be a challenge for some. Physical activity is extremely important to help regulate blood sugar levels, mood, and weight. Limiting simple carbohydrates (in favor of complex carbohydrates in moderation) has been shown to help keep blood sugar in check, too.

Takeaway Message: Your Hormones and Your Sleep

✓ While there are things that women can do to sleep better during the various stages of the life cycle as our hormones fluctuate, we need to understand what is normal for sleep during these different times and what is abnormal.

✓ Sleep changes during different life stages, and there's variation from night to night. Pharmacologic options may be useful to help with hormonal changes, but they are not always indicated.

5.

Other Sleep or Mood Disorders
That Might Look Like Insomnia

Although sleep is more and more in the public consciousness with each passing year, busy primary care doctors and gynecologists have a whole host of things to ask their patients, and sleep problems often fall to the wayside unless the patient mentions it as an issue. While insomnia is a highly prevalent disorder that plagues many women on an all too regular basis, there are some other common sleep disorders that you should review to see if you fit the bill. Form 5.1 at the end of this chapter will help you answer questions about your own sleep issues.

Occasionally when I evaluate women for their reported insomnia, after some questioning it becomes clear that more consultation is needed with a board-certified sleep medicine physician, and likely a sleep study as well. I often see women who are somewhere on the menopausal spectrum with shallow, broken sleep and early morning awakenings. Often they're quite thin and don't meet the typical "overweight male" stereotype of someone with sleep apnea, and when I suggest a sleep study they're almost offended. More frequently than I'd like, the results come back indicating some form of sleep apnea. Although it doesn't always explain the entire sleep issue, it should definitely be addressed as it likely contributes to the awakenings and poor sleep quality.

AM I SLEEPY, OR AM I FATIGUED?

A good starting point for figuring out if another issue is affecting with your sleep is to think about the difference between being fatigued or being sleepy. We often confuse both terms and say we are sleepy when we are indeed fatigued. I like to think of fatigue as that feeling of dragging a ton of bricks behind you, having no energy, no gas in your tank. However, when you try to take a nap or sit quietly on the couch, you are unable to doze. Most women with straight insomnia (meaning no other issue that might be impacting or influencing sleep) commonly say to me, "I wish I could nap, but I just can't even when I try!" In contrast, sleepiness is the actual act of falling asleep, napping, or dozing at times when you are quiet or sedentary and you don't necessarily want to doze.

If you notice a lot of daytime issues with sleepiness—trouble staying awake even when you want to, not just fatigue—consider any of the sleep disorders below or having a discussion with your doctor about anything else that might contribute to your level of sleepiness. If you don't meet any of the criteria for the various sleep disorders below but are still sleepy, it is possible that your insomnia is causing that feeling. However, if you treat the insomnia and are still left feeling sleepy, or the insomnia is just not responding to treatment and your sleepiness worsens, definitely talk with your doctor and consider further evaluation from a physician who is board certified in sleep medicine.

SLEEP APNEA

Sleep apnea is characterized by pauses or a complete cessation of breathing during sleep multiple times throughout the night. Although there are various types of sleep apnea, obstructive sleep apnea (OSA) is the most common form of the disorder. The OSA cycle begins when one falls asleep and the muscles of the airway relax. At some point, they relax so much that breathing is either fully or partially stopped as the tongue or throat collapse into the airway. The brain then senses that there's a lack of oxygen and quickly awakens the sleeper as a protective mechanism. Upon awakening, the muscles of the airway become rigid again and normal breathing is resumed. In most cases, the person with OSA falls right back asleep again, the muscles relax, snoring begins, and another apnea happens, which leads to yet another awakening. This can happen from 5 to 15 times *an hour* in mild cases and over 30 times an hour in severe cases, with some pauses in breathing happening for 10–20 seconds or more! Because the awakenings are quick, most people have no clue that they're having so many apneas throughout the night and are surprised to see the results from their sleep study. The constant awakenings at night can lead to feelings of restless sleep, excessive day-time sleepiness, and occasionally insomnia at times when awakened but unable to return to sleep.

The classic signs of sleep apnea are snoring, choking or gasping, and/or pauses in breathing during sleep. I ironically think of OSA as a "silent" disorder since in many instances the person snoring has no clue that it is indeed happening—instead, the bed partner is the one to bring up the issue! Snoring is extremely common in sleep apnea, but it doesn't always mean one has sleep apnea. Many people who snore don't necessarily have sleep apnea, but some people who don't snore actually do have sleep apnea.

Other common symptoms of sleep apnea include excessive daytime sleepiness, irritability, frequent urination at night, nighttime heartburn, awakenings in the middle of the night (insomnia!), awakening with head-aches in the morning, and restless sleep. You do not need to have all these symptoms to be diagnosed with sleep apnea, but if you have at least some snoring or pauses in breathing during your sleep at night or excessive daytime sleepiness, consider discussing these concerns with your doctor. Form 5.1 at the end of this chapter will help guide you in determining if you might need further evaluation for sleep apnea.

Although women usually report having these issues once asked in detail, they are more likely to talk with their doctor about more vague symptoms than the classic apnea symptoms of snoring and choking/gasping in sleep: insomnia, morning headaches, depression, lack of energy, and sleepiness. These complaints can often lead the doctor to investigate other medical and psychiatric disorders, not typically sleep apnea. As a result, sleep apnea is frequently misdiagnosed as cardiac illness, health anxiety, fibromyalgia, anemia, depression, fatigue, stress, hypertension, hypothyroidism, perimenopause, and yes, insomnia. This doesn't mean that you can't have several of these diagnoses at once, but sometimes things like uncontrolled high blood pressure or morning headaches are caused by sleep apnea, and figuring out the root issue (not breathing properly during sleep!) can properly address the other medical problems. Sometimes, just treating the sleep apnea can deepen sleep as it reduces the awakenings due to apneas. And other times, combining CBT-I with the recommended treatment for OSA—most commonly some form of a PAP (positive airway pressure) machine—is best. Many effective treatments are available for sleep apnea; a sleep physician can help guide you to the right one if OSA is an issue.

One other important thing to note is that, if you suspect you have sleep apnea but are currently taking sedating medications for issues such as anxiety or sleep, many of these medications can further relax the muscles of the airway, thereby worsening sleep apnea. Sometimes this can lead to waking up feeling even worse, even though having thought you slept all night. If you possibly have apnea and are taking sedating medications (or even drinking alcohol at night), you may be worsening your apnea without even knowing it. The best recommendation here is to properly treat the apnea; then, once it is under control, speak with your doctor about using sedating medications at bedtime. You may even find that you won't need them as much with the use of CBT-I.

OSA is one of the most common sleep disorders in the United States, affecting over 20 million adults, with most cases actually going undiagnosed or untreated. Many people do not realize the deleterious long-term effects of sleep apnea and let it continue, or try to treat some of the symptoms of the disorder (depression, excessive sleepiness, awakenings at night) without actually treating the underlying cause of the problem. Aside from daytime sleepiness and concentration/attention issues, OSA has been linked to an increased risk of stroke, high blood pressure, and cardiac issues. It should not be ignored, as many effective treatments are available based on the type and severity of the apnea.

The population-based Study of Women's Health Across the Nation (SWAN) found a 20 percent rate of sleep apnea (moderate and severe levels) in perimenopausal and postmenopausal women, compared to 4 percent of premenopausal women (Hall, Matthews & Kravitz, 2009). Some groups of women are at an increased risk of developing sleep apnea, including those who are postmenopausal and/or obese. Women with PCOS also have significantly higher rates of OSA compared to women without the disorder. It has typically been thought that the rates of sleep apnea among women are far lower than among men, but this gap is closing over time as more and more physicians are beginning to recognize the signs of sleep apnea in women and refer them for sleep studies and treatment. Given the increase in sleep apnea rates in menopausal women, the rates between men and women begin to even out with age.

Significant increases in OSA are also seen in pregnant women, and if you notice any of the symptoms noted above, definitely bring it up with your ob-gyn and consider seeking a consultation with a board-certified physician in sleep medicine. Research has shown that routine weekly snoring increases from around 10 percent in the first trimester to 20 percent in the third trimester, with excessive sleepiness increasing significantly as well (Balserak, 2015) There are a number of reasons for this occurrence, including increased weight gain, older age while pregnant, narrowing of the airway due to increased estrogen and progesterone, and pregnancy rhinitis (nasal congestion not simply due to allergies). Make sure to get proper treatment for pregnancy-related OSA, as research has linked it with gestational diabetes, pre-eclampsia, and slowed fetal growth (Balserak, 2015).

RESTLESS LEGS SYNDROME

Restless legs syndrome (RLS), also known as Willis-Ekbom disease, is a sleep disorder that typically interferes with the ability to fall asleep. People with RLS often describe the symptoms in varying ways, but the most common symptom is a nearly irresistible urge to move the arms or legs (it doesn't need to be only in the legs!). Some people describe the sensations as pins and needles, creepy crawly feelings, or itchiness. RLS follows a circadian pattern, meaning that it worsens as the night grows closer but is not typically present during the daytime hours. These uncomfortable feelings are worse when at rest, especially when sitting down or lying in bed. People with RLS typically have to get up, move around, and stretch to find relief, worsening the ability to fall asleep. For some people it is a mild nuisance, but for others it can be disabling, given how uncomfortable it can be and how much it can interfere with falling asleep.

RLS is relatively common, affecting about 10 percent of the U.S. population. While people of any age, even children, are diagnosed with RLS, it is more common in older adults and women. Younger people with RLS are typically misdiagnosed as having "growing pains" or muscle soreness when in fact it is RLS. It is thought to be genetic in most cases. RLS is frequently seen in pregnant women after the 20-week mark (I had it myself with both pregnancies!)—make sure to bring it up to your ob-gyn if it is causing problems with your ability to sleep.

A number of medical problems can also lead to RLS, including iron deficiency (easy to test for and treat if necessary), diabetes, peripheral neuropathy, rheumatoid arthritis, Parkinson's disease, and renal disease. Antidepressants, certain antinausea medications, and antihistamines can also cause RLS. Talk with your doctor if you think any of these things may be impacting your sleep. Form 5.1 at the end of this chapter will help guide you in determining if you might need further evaluation for RLS. Effective treatments are available for many people with RLS; you needn't suffer in silence.

PERIODIC LIMB MOVEMENT DISORDER

Periodic limb movement disorder (PLMD) is a repetitive movement of the limbs (typically the legs, though it can occur in the upper body) during sleep, often seen on a sleep study as jerking movements and flexing of the foot and ankle or knee and hip at regular intervals every 20–40 seconds. Most patients are completely unaware of the jerking movements during sleep; instead, a bed partner typically reports that the patient is moving a lot during the night and kicks in bed. Another common sign is messy sheets in the morning from moving around a lot at night.

Most people with RLS have PLMD, but not vice versa, and many people with PLMD don't actually go for treatment because they aren't aware it is an issue. If the movements are problematic enough, they can lead to daytime fatigue and sleepiness, irritability, and broken nighttime sleep. On occasion, I've had women who were treated for their insomnia using CBT-I and began sleeping through the night but still felt excessively tired and even sometimes sleepy during the day. They slept alone and didn't have anyone to corroborate kicking during sleep. A sleep study would show PLMD, explaining why a solid night of sleep felt unrefreshing. Medication is typically the first-line treatment for PLMD, and it is quite effective in most cases. Form 5.1 at the end of this chapter will help you determine if PLMD contributes to your sleep issues.

CIRCADIAN RHYTHM SLEEP DISORDERS

The hallmark of a circadian rhythm sleep disorder (CRSD) is when you have trouble with sleep on a regular basis, but when on your own clock and with no pressures to have to go to sleep or wake up at a specified time, you can sleep a full night. Essentially, people with CRSDs can sleep fine on their own schedule, but the sleep schedule they *need* to keep doesn't usually fit well with what their bodies do. Common forms of CRSD include delayed sleep-phase disorder (DSPD; aka night owl syndrome), advanced sleep-phase disorder (ASPD; aka early bird syndrome), extreme jet lag, and shift work sleep disorder. Form 5.1 at the end of this chapter will help guide you in determining if you might need further evaluation for some type of CRSD, as described below.

DSPD is very often seen in teenagers and young adults but can linger far into adulthood and create issues for awakening. In DSPD, you struggle with going to bed early because you're just not biologically ready to go to sleep yet. This, to the untrained eye, looks like classic insomnia at the beginning of the night. However, once you finally fall asleep you stay asleep just fine, but then you struggle to wake up early in the morning for work or school since the amount of time asleep was limited. Treatments for DSPD differ from straightforward CBT-I interventions and should be addressed with a trained sleep specialist who can shift circadian rhythms using strategically timed low-dose melatonin, gradual delay of sleep and wake schedules, or even light therapy. Don't play around with a light box or randomly taking melatonin for this issue—timing and dosage are key to fixing the underlying circadian issue, hence the recommendation to work with a trained sleep specialist.

ASPD is similar in nature to DSPD but in the opposite direction. More often seen in older adults, people with ASPD go to bed very early, only to awaken very early, in the middle of the night. When looking at total sleep time at night, it is completely within normal limits, just shifted much earlier than one would typically like. These patients often complain to physicians of awakening too early in the morning but not being able to return to sleep again. Far too often, no one asks them, "What time did you go to sleep at night?" If the answer was 8 p.m. (or something like that) and they had a full night of sleep, it is likely ASPD. Treatments are similar to those for DSPD, again, strategically timed with the help of a sleep doctor.

Shift work is a tough adjustment for many people. If you find that you're struggling with getting a good night's sleep on your nights off or are unable to sleep during the daytime hours on workdays, consider talking with a sleep doctor about available treatments. Light therapy, medication, and behavioral interventions are all necessary to help one acclimate to shift work.

NARCOLEPSY

Narcolepsy is a chronic neurological disorder that impacts the brain's control over sleep and wake states. Autoimmune and genetic factors are more and more implicated in its cause, and although there is no cure as of yet, a number of effective treatments are now available to manage the symptoms of the disorder. It is extremely misunderstood, underrecognized, and often stigmatized in society. Although it is uncommon, it is not as rare as one might think: 1 in every 2,000 people has narcolepsy. The hallmark symptom that all people with narcolepsy have, excessive daytime sleepiness, can be debilitating for many.

Another symptom seen in many, but not all, people with narcolepsy is cataplexy—a sudden loss of muscle tone and weakness while awake that is triggered by strong, sudden emotions like laughter, anger, excitement, fear, or stress. The muscle weakness can be extremely subtle, such as a drooping of an eyelid or corner of the mouth, but it can also be quite extreme, like buckling of the knees. Cataplexy is not usually seen in other medical or psychiatric disorders (occasionally seen as a medication side effect), and if you have this issue, definitely consider mentioning it to your primary care doctor. Form 5.1 at the end of this chapter will help guide you in determining if you have other symptoms related to narcolepsy that might need further evaluation.

Another common symptom of narcolepsy is insomnia and broken nighttime sleep. I've occasionally been sent patients who report nighttime sleep disruption and excessive daytime sleepiness and standard insomnia treatments just weren't working, and it turned out that narcolepsy was the cause of their broken nighttime sleep.

Other common symptoms of narcolepsy include sleep paralysis (a seconds-long inability to move or speak when falling asleep or awakening), hallucinations (typically visual) solely around falling asleep and waking up, and automatic behaviors: temporary sleep episodes where you're engaged in a habitual behavior, for a few seconds or minutes, with no conscious awareness of actually doing it.

Since it is so misunderstood and many medical professionals do not have much training in narcolepsy, patients often wait over a decade before getting an accurate diagnosis. They are frequently misdiagnosed as having a psychiatric disorder such as depression, bipolar disorder, or even psychosis. However, thanks to the work of narcolepsy researchers and patient advocacy groups, doctors are becoming more aware of the diagnostic red flags and catching symptoms earlier and earlier.

"BUT I DON'T WANT A SLEEP STUDY!"

Before you stop and say "I don't want to have a sleep study—I'll never sleep in that sleep lab with all those things on me!," let me say that sleep studies today have come a long way from where they once were. For many straightforward sleep apnea cases, a significant number of sleep centers are now doing home sleep studies, meaning that they send you home with a simple sleep monitoring device that will track your sleep. Some are more sensitive than others, but most will, at the very least, measure your breathing (usually with a chest band) and pulse oximetry (the finger clip that measures your oxygen levels) throughout the night. Others have a simple cap to put on that will give your doctor a sense of sleep staging as well. Often, insurance will dictate if someone can have a sleep study at home or not, but more and more sleep doctors are using home studies to get sleep data while the patient is sleeping in a more comfortable setting. We don't expect a perfect night of sleep on a sleep study. Even if you sleep in the lab, just sleep as best you can—even if you sleep only a few hours, it often produces enough data to help the doctor see if any apnea is present and what might be necessary for treatment.

A sleep study is not currently indicated just for insomnia—all it shows us is that you're lying in bed awake at night! However, if you think there's any other medical issue or sleep disorder that might be impacting your sleep, awakenings, or the quality of your sleep, definitely have a talk with your doctor and consider having a sleep study. It could lead to some really enlightening information and improve your quality of life.

MOOD DISORDERS AND INSOMNIA

Women have higher rates of depression and anxiety than do men, and to ignore any sleep component would be a mistake in treating an overall mood disorder. As I hope I made abundantly clear in previous chapters, you don't have to think of a mood disorder as always being the root cause of your insomnia, requiring sole treatment to fix your sleep problems. This "primary" and "secondary" way of thinking about disorders only serves to maintain the insomnia for many women, thereby delaying treatment for the sleep disorder even more. If you suffer from consistent feelings of sadness, down mood, or lack of interest in things you usually enjoy, for 2 weeks or more, talk with your doctor about being evaluated for depression. And if you're also suffering from insomnia, consider treating that as well. Sometimes, just sleeping better can improve your mood overall.

We know that even if depression is properly treated, any lingering insomnia increases the risk of depression relapse. Insomnia has been found to worsen depression symptoms and even increase the risk of suicide in those with depression. If you have any thoughts or feelings of wanting to hurt yourself or someone else, please contact your doctor, therapist, or psychiatrist for help. If you feel that you are an imminent danger to yourself or someone else or have thoughts or plans to act out on your suicidal or homicidal thoughts, call 911 or go to your local emergency room—don't wait.

The same goes for anxiety and insomnia—having an anxiety disorder is not a reason to avoid treating your insomnia, since working on the anxiety first doesn't routinely alleviate the insomnia. In fact, insomnia increases the risk of developing anxiety; even just having one night of poor sleep heightens anxiety the next day.

While using CBT-I in the realm of postpartum depression and anxiety is still quite new, data suggest that improving sleep helps improve mood symptoms in people with these conditions. It is still extremely important to note any feelings of depression, sadness, irritability, or anxiety to your ob-gyn, as medication or talk therapy may be indicated for a mood issue as well as insomnia—you do not want postpartum depression or anxiety to go unrecognized.

Takeaway Message: Sleep Disorders

✓ Many sleep disorders can also look like insomnia. Form 5.1 can help you evaluate whether you want to consider a consultation to rule out any other sleep disorders that might look like insomnia.

✓ With the growing rates of sleep apnea and RLS especially in women, make sure to rule out any symptoms that might require a separate medical treatment and possible sleep study.

✓ If you think that you have depression or anxiety that is not likely to improve with just improving your sleep, talk with your doctor about adding in treatment for that issue.

✓ Treating the sleep problem alone may reduce the severity of co-occurring mood disorders, but keep a close eye on any worsening (or remaining) depression and/or anxiety during and after implementing treatment strategies.

FORM 5.1: Should I Be Evaluated for Another Sleep Disorder?

Check the appropriate boxes below. If you answer yes to any of the following symptoms, consider talking with your doctor for further evaluation.

Snoring and sleep apnea	Yes	No
Do you snore loudly, or have you been told you snore loudly?		
Do you ever awaken choking, gasping, or gulping for air? Do you awaken yourself with snorting or gasping noises?		
Do you often awaken with a dry mouth or sore throat?		
Do you frequently awaken with headaches?		
Do you use the bathroom frequently (more than twice) at night?		
Do you feel like your nighttime sleep is unrefreshing even when you get a full night's sleep?		
Do you have frequent acid indigestion or heartburn?		
Do you feel sleepy or sluggish and find it difficult to stay awake during inactive or quiet situations?		
Restless legs syndrome (Willis-Ekbom disease)	**Yes**	**No**
Do you find it is difficult to fall asleep at night because of uncontrollable or unusual urges to move your legs or arms when sedentary?		
Do you find this urge worsens as the night comes closer?		
Periodic limb movement disorder	**Yes**	**No**
Do you ever experience twitching or jerking of your legs while asleep?		
Do you wake up in the morning with your sheets in a mess?		
Do you awaken after a full night's sleep feeling unrested, sleepy, and/or fatigued?		

Circadian rhythm disorder	Yes	No
If you didn't have to keep specific hours (such as getting up or going to sleep at a specific time because of school, family, or work), do you think you would be able to get a full, uninterrupted night's sleep on your own time clock on a daily basis?		
Do you work the night shift or irregular shifts that makes it difficult for you to obtain a good night of sleep?		
Other sleep disorder symptoms to evaluate		
When you fall asleep or wake up, have you had trouble moving your arms and legs even though you tried?		
Have you experienced sudden muscle weakness while awake brought on by an intense emotion?		
Do you have recurrent/frequent nightmares?		
Do you sleepwalk? Sleep eat? Sleep talk?		
Have you ever injured yourself while in your sleep or fallen out of bed in your sleep?		

6.

Cognitive Behavioral Therapy for Insomnia

C BT-I is essentially a grouping of various treatment techniques that have been shown to be effective for insomnia. Parts 2 and 3 of this book each focus in detail on making changes that have been shown effective for improving insomnia symptoms. Each technique has solid evidence behind it; some strategies are more effective for some women than for others. Combining them to get more "bang for your buck" is essentially the basis of CBT-I.

The cognitive approaches (the "C" in CBT) address how cognitions (aka thoughts) negatively impact your sleep. Strategies to combat worry and quiet the brain are discussed in Part 3. The behavioral techniques (the "B" in CBT) in Part 2 address how to track your sleep, basic good sleep practices (aka sleep hygiene), reassociating the bed only with sleep, and adjusting your sleep/wake schedule based on how much sleep you are currently getting, as reported on your sleep diary. The behavioral strategies tend to have the most robust evidence behind them, and I always start my patients with the behavioral techniques outlined in this book. I work with my patients to problem solve the behavioral strategies and then move on to cognitive interventions to help quiet the mind and reduce worry about obtaining sleep and/or the consequences of not getting a good night's sleep.

Although each strategy discussed here has its own evidence behind it on an individual level, when combined as a treatment package, CBT-I has a robust amount of data showing that it works for many women with insomnia, across a vast array of sleep issues. Although these strategies can be used alone by many people with insomnia, a combined approach gives you more bang for your buck at the outset. The choice is up to you to start with more or fewer approaches in the beginning.

If you're concerned about making too many changes at once, or worry that change may be difficult from the start, remember that you've likely had insomnia for quite some time, and it may be tough at first. Patience and consistency lead to behavior change. If you're feeling overwhelmed with making big changes to your sleep patterns, consider starting with just tracking your sleep. Once you're good at tracking, think about adding in stimulus control for a week or two. When stimulus control is under your belt, then add in sleep restriction. The individual strategies of this book combine very nicely and can be done together at the outset or gradually introduced one at a time, depending on your level of comfort and motivation. Whatever you decide to do, just try to be consistent with the strategy you've chosen, to give your body time to adjust and see if it is working and whether you need to add in another module.

HOW WELL DOES CBT-I WORK?

Compared to various sleep medications, CBT-I has been shown to be equally as effective in the short term, but it outshines medications in the long term. Simply put, you can take medication night after night to help you sleep, but after one or two nights without the medication, the insomnia typically returns. That's why I often end up seeing women in my office. The prospect of relying on a sleep aid when other options are just as effective is often what drives people to try CBT-I.

Some research has looked at combining sleep aids with CBT-I at the beginning of treatment. While the results suggest a mild to modest gain in sleep from the initial combination of the two strategies, Morin et al. (2009) showed that the best longer-term benefits were found when CBT-I was continued and medications were stopped after the first 6 weeks. So, the bigger question here is whether you want to initially use medication, and run the risk of attributing all of your gains in your sleep to a pill, or start out thinking that you yourself have the power to make changes to your sleep.

When you start doing CBT-I, it might not work as immediately as taking a sleep aid, but once you stop going to sessions with a CBT-I practitioner (or you stop actively doing treatment yourself with this book), as you're doing better and are maintaining those gains, you will have the tools to continue sleeping well, without taking medications. And the best part is that when the occasional bad night pops up in the future, as it normally does for us all, you will know what to do to help keep things in check so you likely won't develop long-term chronic insomnia again.

CBT-I has been shown to be very effective even at 3-year follow-ups in patients with both depression and insomnia, even more effective than depression treatment alone. It makes sense, right? Many people can become quite depressed about not sleeping, and improving sleep in the long term can help improve mood. Even Web-based CBT-I programs have shown promising results that continue one or more years after treatment ends.

Since there has been such robust evidence in favor of CBT-I, the American Academy of Sleep Medicine considers this treatment to be the first-line intervention for chronic insomnia (Schutte-Rodin, Broch, Buysse, Dorsey, Sateia et al., 2008). Even more notable, in 2016 the American College of Physicians indicated that CBT-I should be the first-line treatment for *all* adults with insomnia (Brasure et al., 2016). This was a major shift in the way that insomnia treatment was viewed in internal medicine, as pharmaceutical sleep aids were frequently prescribed over CBT-I. And "best practice" guidelines for obstetrics give CBT-I high marks (Abbott, Attarian, & Zee, 2014).

You might be asking yourself, then, *If CBT-I is so effective and recommended by major medical groups, why did my doctor not suggest it to me?* There could be a number of reasons for this, but typically it's because most doctors simply aren't familiar with where to send a patient for CBT-I. As common as chronic insomnia is, there sadly aren't enough skilled treatment providers in this field. Although it is often ideal to receive CBT-I on a one-on-one basis with a sleep clinician like myself, it actually isn't always necessary. There's really solid data out there suggesting that it works over the phone, online, or even from self-help books like this.

We also know that CBT-I works in varying populations. It has been shown effective for insomnia in older adults, younger adults, cancer, anxiety, depression, multiple sclerosis, fibromyalgia, chronic pain, and many other conditions. In summary, it works for a lot of women in various medical and psychiatric situations, is often just as effective as the medications, and usually outperforms medications in the long run.

Over the past 10 or so years, insomnia treatment research has slowly begun to focus specifically on women, especially given their susceptibility to spikes in sleep disorders during hormonal changes such as pregnancy, the postpartum period, and the transition into menopause. Sleep problems are extremely common in perimenopausal women, with many reporting issues with awakenings in the middle of the night and early morning. Often, these awakenings involve hot flashes, making it extremely hard for women to return to sleep. CBT-I was often thought of as being insufficient as a standalone treatment for women suffering from hot flashes related to menopause, who were considered to required medical intervention such as low-dose hormone replacement.

However, this is not actually always the case and was one of my main reasons for writing this book. Some newer data from the MsFLASH (Menopause Strategies: Finding Lasting Answers for Symptoms and Health) study (McCurry et al., 2016) suggests that CBT-I is indeed effective for perimenopausal women suffering from hot flashes. In fact, when the study compared only six phone-delivered CBT-I sessions with other treatments, such as antidepressants, yoga/exercise, omega-3 fish oil, or hormones, CBT-I was the superior option. Women who engaged in CBT-I had fewer awakenings and deeper sleep, even when they were frequently awakened by hot flashes. This study only further confirms the American College of Physicians' suggestion that CBT-I should be the first-line treatment for insomnia in almost all patients. If CBT-I is then found to be ineffective or cannot be administered or followed for various reasons, then we move onto other options, such as prescribed or over-the-counter medication or lifestyle changes.

Although data are not necessarily abundant as of yet, initial research in use of CBT-I for both prenatal and postnatal insomnia has been promising. Sleep loss during pregnancy (especially the last trimester) is extremely common and often considered to be a normal part of the process. However, significant chronic sleep disruption during pregnancy has been associated with several negative outcomes, including preeclampsia, preterm labor, gestational diabetes, and depression. When given a choice between CBT-I and pharmacotherapy for their insomnia, pregnant women have indicated a preference for CBT-I (Sedov, Goodman, Tomfohr-Madsen, 2017). Research in pregnant women is often lacking, and this is one area where it truly is needed. Tomfohr-Madsen, Clayborne, Rouleau, and Campbell (2017) investigated five sessions of group CBT-I in 13 women and noted significant reductions in insomnia symptoms and improved sleep quality. As an added benefit, they noted reduced depression, anxiety related to pregnancy, and overall fatigue as treatment progressed.

Another area where CBT-I has been studied is in postpartum women who stuffer from insomnia despite their babies beginning to sleep more consolidated stretches at night. CBT-I has been shown effective as well for these patients, even with just a few sessions at a time, when getting out of the house or keeping some sense of a schedule or structure might seem nearly impossible. This is yet another area where women do not always speak up about their insomnia, or they think that poor sleep is a natural part of having a baby in the house. Yes, to some extent, sleep disruption is a natural part of the process, but only for the first few months; then it shouldn't be dirsrupted anymore. Once the baby begins sleeping better, the mom ideally should as well.

Even during the early months, many new moms find it difficult to sleep soundly between the baby's awakenings and are hesitant to use sleep aids (over the counter and/or prescribed) due to breastfeeding and wanting to be alert enough to tend to a baby on an unpredictable schedule. This is another area where CBT-I shows a lot of promise: a few research teams have demonstrated success with CBT-I with postpartum women in as few as five weekly treatment sessions (Swanson, Flynn, Adams-Mundy, Armitage and Arnedt, 2013). More work is clearly needed in this area, but what we have found from the initial studies on CBT-I during pregnancy and the postpartum period is quite promising.

Although CBT-I works for so many people and with very few side effects compared to over-the-counter and prescription sleep medications, it doesn't work for everyone, or it doesn't always work *enough* for some. For those cases, in Chapter 14 guest author Dr. Katherine Takayasu briefly addresses alternative treatments to consider and discuss with your doctor, including hormonal treatments, over-the-counter sleep aids, prescription sleep aids, supplements, acupuncture, and many others. The main focus of this book is on CBT-I, and if that's not enough for you, there are other treatments to try, often in combination with CBT-I.

Takeaway Message: Cognitive Behavioral Therapy for Insomnia

✓ CBT-I is a combination of a core set of strategies to combat insomnia.

✓ Some people find it is best to do all the strategies at the start, to get the most robust effect at the beginning, whereas others feel it is easier to gradually introduce one after another—go with your comfort level and what works in your life.

✓ CBT-I is highly effective for people of all ages, for both women and men.

PART 2

Change Your
Behaviors

7.

Track Your Sleep

hallmark of cognitive therapy is to consider all available evidence around us and look at our lives in a very methodical, scientific way. Our thoughts and feelings about our surroundings are occasionally colored by the tinted lenses through which we view life. Just because we have a thought doesn't always mean it is 100 percent true. That's not to say that it is true, or that it is false—we just need to evaluate the evidence behind it in order to move forward.

This is particularly important when looking at the quality and patterns of our sleep. We all fall prey to believing our own thoughts, which might not always be true. Some examples: "I always have trouble falling asleep," or "It takes me hours to get back to sleep each night," or "I don't think exercise makes any difference whatsoever to my sleep." These are very black-and-white thoughts—they may be true, but in reality, we often forget about the nights that were really somewhere in the middle.

People with insomnia (and, let's be honest, even those without sleep problems) often minimize the better nights, frequently dismissing the sufficient, "just fine" nights, maximizing the worst nights, and focusing on those times when sleep just didn't come and the next day's effects were rough. In addition, we may also focus on the opposite side, maximizing not only the really bad nights but also the amazingly good ones, too, therefore romanticizing the idea that "the only days I felt OK were after getting a solid 8 hours of sleep."

Why is this important to think about? Because CBT is about investigating your own sleep patterns, gathering data, and then working to making changes and evaluating how these changes help improve your sleep over time. The best way to do this is through tracking your sleep with a sleep diary.

Tracking certain behaviors can yield a lot of information about patterns and even lead to behavior change. For example, if you're interested in losing weight, simply tracking your food intake for a week can give you a lot of data on the various foods you eat, the quantities, what times you might eat more processed foods, and any triggers to poor eating. Just gaining that information from a diary and analyzing the results can lead to behavior change in some patients. Tracking tends to bring your attention to your thoughts and behavior patterns, therefore leading to change. The same goes for routinely tracking your sleep with a diary.

Using a sleep diary will help you see the subtle, or not so subtle, variations your sleep from night to night with. It also helps keep you honest with how well you adhere to the treatment suggestions in this book, and helps you know when to make changes in your sleep/wake schedule as your sleep changes over time. Tracking your sleep can also uncover any patterns that might impact your nighttime sleep. For example, you may not have noticed, but your sleep diary might indicate that you take longer to fall asleep on the days you had a coffee after 4 p.m., or you wake up earlier in the morning when you go to bed earlier. Some notice that exercising too close to bed might make their sleep lighter, or that having an extra glass of wine an hour before bed leads to more awakenings at night. I frequently see women notice that their sleep is more disrupted on nights after a particularly stressful day. These are all patterns that can be uncovered with a sleep diary.

Before filling out a sleep diary, it is extremely important to understand that the key to properly doing one is, oddly, to not look at a clock. Yes, you read that right. *Do not look at the clock!* Many people then ask, "How will I know how long I was awake, how long I actually slept? It won't be accurate." Interestingly enough, it doesn't really matter exactly how long your awakenings are—what matters is your perception. If you perceive that you were up for 2 hours in the middle of the night, your ratings of how long you think you were up are actually quite internally consistent from night to night. It might not be exactly 2 hours, but it'll be *your* 2 hours. And if I asked you night after night how long you think you were awake, your estimate would be quite consistent overall.

What is more important is that we see overall weekly changes in your perceptions of how long you *think* you were awake each night. If we see that you were often up for, on average, 3 hours each night throughout the week, and then that starts to drop to an average of 1.5 hours per night, we know that you think you are awake less throughout the night and likely improving.

More and more, I see women come to my office for a consultation without sleep diaries and instead with printouts from a smart watch or app that tracks sleep data. Although, at the time of the writing of this book, technology is definitely improving from year to year, it isn't yet perfect. I have found that it often leads those with insomnia to become hyperfocused on their sleep, analyzing what nights were "good" and "bad." Remember, these apps and watches typically estimate sleep based on your nighttime movement, and sometimes we move during our sleep, or we stay completely still when we're awake in the hope of fall asleep. As a result, sleep/wake times may not be completely accurate all of the time. While there is definitely a place for these trackers in making people aware of their sleep, at present I don't typically recommend them for patients with insomnia since the goal of insomnia treatment is to eventually become *less* focused on your sleep, something that was usually the case before the insomnia ever developed. A study by Baron, Abbott, Jao, Manalo and Mullen (2017) looked at the use of these sleep trackers with insomnia patients, and they found that worries about insomnia and focus on sleep increased when trackers were introduced.

Properly tracking your sleep can give you lots of information regarding any patterns related to poor sleep (or even disprove any preconceived notions regarding your sleep). Before you begin the treatment strategies in this book, the best first step is to take out the sleep diary in this book (Form 7.1). Make some extra copies of the diary and earnestly fill it out every evening and morning for at least 2 week, ideally 2 weeks.

Whenever I see a woman in my practice, I always ask that she fill out this sleep diary for the 2 weeks before we meet. Why not just a few days? There is individual variation from night to night regarding sleep, and stressors can happen from time to time as well. A solid 2 weeks of tracking your sleep can show you realistic sleep averages overall, taking into account any short-term stressors and nightly variation. There are many types of sleep diaries, and even a simple Internet search can be overwhelming. There are smartphone apps with sleep diaries and websites where you can log in data on a daily basis. The reality, though, is that a sleep diary is easy to do yourself, without any additional technology. Just take the diary from this book, make multiple copies, and keep one fresh copy per week in your room.

COMPLETING YOUR SLEEP DIARY: THE BASICS

Refer to the baseline sleep diary (Form 7.1). It is in your best interest to fill out your sleep diary just before you go to bed and right after you wake up each morning. If you forget to fill in a day or two, don't bother recreating the information at a later time. Chances are it will not be as accurate as when you fill it in right when you go to bed or get up. If you spend more than one or two minutes a night and morning completing it, you're doing something wrong. Your sleep diary should be a quick snapshot of your sleep/wake behaviors; you do not need lots of detailed information.

Notice that the sleep diary in this book is divided into three major sections: a section to fill out just before going to bed, one to fill out the next morning, and a section for calculating your sleep stats. Just before you go to bed for the night, fill out the top section of the diary—remember, this should only take a minute. Then, when you wake up in the morning for good, fill out the middle section of the diary. At the end of each week, complete the bottom section to average your sleep quantity for the week and generate an overall picture of how you're doing on a week-to-week basis.

An important caveat here is to *not fill out the diary throughout the night*. Tracking your sleep with every awakening at night is quite possibly one of the worst things you can do, since it makes you look at the clock at night and become hyperfocused on how many times you woke up, as well as for how long you have been awake. One of the goals of insomnia treatment is to have you think *less* about your sleep overall—just as you probably were not too focused on it in the past, before your sleep problems began. Tracking every single awakening at night or watching the clock serves the exact opposite purpose. I prefer you keep the sleep diary either just outside of your room or on a bureau across from your bed, not on your nightstand next to your bed where you might be thinking too much about it.

As for any concerns about whether you might forget in the morning just how often or how long you were awake the night before, try to let those worries go and estimate as best as possible. Again, what we are more focused on here is your *perception* of how long or how often you were awake at night.

Below I describe how to use each section of the sleep diary. Form 7.2 shows an example diary that a fictitious patient, Ruth, used to calculate her baseline sleep patterns. You can refer to that for examples of how to fill out the different sections.

The Top Section: Fill Out Just Before Going to Bed

A. *Day and date:* This one sounds pretty self-explanatory, but it is surprising how easy it is to become confused. Since you are filling out the top part of the log just before you go to bed, put down that date. For example, if you are about to go to bed for the night on Monday, April 10, write 4/10 as the date. Then, when you get up in the morning (Tuesday, 4/11), fill out the middle section for 4/10, thinking about the night that you just had (from late 4/10 into 4/11 early morning hours).

B. *Naps:* Think about the day you just had as you're filling out your sleep diary. Did you take any naps? If so, how long were they for, and when in the day did they happen? Also, try to record any dozing sessions when you may have unintentionally nodded off. A common example would be falling asleep in front of the television at night before bedtime. Write it down even if it was just a 2–3 minute doze—this information may prove very useful in your overall treatment, as small dozes can greatly impact your sleep!

C. *Exercise:* Write down the time and type of exercise. Make note of any purposeful exercise, not just walking a lot to catch the bus.

D. *Caffeine:* Note any caffeine you had that day, making sure to write down the type (coffee, green tea, etc.), time, and amount you consumed. Keep in mind that caffeine isn't only in coffee. Chocolate and certain types of tea and soda contain caffeine as well. Do not assume tea or coffee is decaffeinated; make sure it says so on the label. If not, write it down.

E. *Sleep medications or alcohol:* This one is rather self-explanatory as well. Note any alcohol you had, as well as the estimated amount and time consumed. Same thing for any sleep medication: write down everything that you took for the purposes of inducing sleep (both over-the-counter and prescribed). Also make a note of the dose you took. Remember, it is important not to mix alcohol with sleep medication, as it can be quite dangerous.

F. *Time you went to bed and turned out the lights:* Ideally, you should be getting in bed when you are sleepy and want to go to sleep for the night. Here you should write down the time that you actually got in bed with the intention of going to sleep for the night.

The Middle Section: Complete in the Morning in Reference to the Night Before

A. *Time to fall asleep for the first time:* This part of the diary is where patients tend to get stuck. As discussed earlier, just estimate here. Once you turned out the lights, how long did it take you to fall asleep? Five minutes? Three hours?

B. *Number of awakenings in the middle of the night:* How often do you think you woke up? Do not include your final awakening here.

C. *Total time awake after falling asleep:* Combine all the times you think you were awake in the middle of the night (*after* you first fell asleep), estimating how long you think you were awake *in total*. For example, if you woke up three times in the middle of the night, each for 20 minutes, write down 60 minutes in this column (3 times awake × 20 minutes each = 60 minutes).

D. *Time you finally woke up:* Note when you think you were done sleeping for good. If it was before the time you are supposed to awaken for the morning, just estimate here.

E. *Time you finally got out of bed:* Even though you might be awake, you may have continued to lie in bed. Note the time you finally got up and out of bed without any plans to get back into bed.

The Bottom Section: Synthesize Your Sleep Stats

This section averages your sleep quantity for the week and helps you generate an overall picture of how you're doing on a week-to-week basis, understanding that there is variation across nights. Although some people fill out the sleep stats on a daily basis, I much prefer that you wait until the end of the week to complete the section, helping reduce focus on whether each night was up to certain standards. We're more interested in how you're doing *on average* across the week, and if you are hyperfocused on how much sleep you obtained each night, that excessive focus on total sleep time can actually worsen your insomnia, as you may put undue pressure on yourself to try to sleep more.

One of the most robust treatment modules of CBT-I is sleep restriction. Although a detailed discussion appears later in this book (see Chapter 10), for current purposes you'll need to know your sleep stats in order to tailor your own sleep restriction program later. We need to know your *total sleep time* and your *sleep efficiency*, both averaged across a week's time.

Total sleep time (TST) is pretty self-explanatory: how many hours and minutes you were asleep each night, averaged at the end of the week. It is a measure of the quantity of sleep you obtained at night. Sleep efficiency percentage (SE%), on the other hand, looks much more at the consolidation of your sleep throughout the night, with the idea that more *compressed sleep* (aka more continuous sleep) at night is better than short intervals of sleep on and off. Believe it or not, more is not always better when it comes to sleep. SE% lets us know what percentage of the night you were in bed actually asleep.

For example, if I went right to bed, fell asleep immediately, slept straight through the night and woke up to my alarm clock in the morning, I would have an SE% of 100 percent. If I went to bed but didn't sleep at all the entire night and tossed and turned until my alarm went off in the morning, I would have an SE% of 0 percent. Both of these numbers are highly unusual, and although many people strive for a "perfect" 100 percent SE%, it is actually quite abnormal and suggests that you might be too sleepy for varying reasons.

We want to aim for *at least* 85 percent on average across the week, suggesting that you take a short while to fall asleep and maybe awaken a bit in the middle of the night or just before getting up in the morning— all within normal limits. And remember, as I've said before, there's individual variation in your sleep from night to night, so what we try to aim for is an *average* SE% of at least 85 percent over five nights. This accounts for mostly good nights and a few rougher ones each week.

Calculating SE% and sleep restriction might seem daunting at first to some people who are math-phobic (cue my own hand high in the air), but it is actually quite simple. Once you get the hang of it, it will provide a nice, guided framework for you to change your bedtime from week to week as your sleep changes, ideally for the better. The first thing you need to do is know your baseline numbers in order to initiate sleep restriction.

It is much easier to get these concepts by using an example sleep diary. In the following description I refer to the bottom section of Ruth's example diary (Form 7.2) to demonstrate how simple it is to calculate these stats.

Step 1. Calculate Total Time in Bed (TIB). For each column, look at what time you went to bed at night and what time you woke up in the morning. Calculate how many hours and minutes you were in bed (ignore any time you got out of and back into bed throughout the night), and then convert it completely into minutes by multiplying the hours by 60 minutes. Put that value in the appropriate column for the night in the TIB row.

In Ruth's baseline sleep diary (Form 7.2), you can see that for the Monday 6/24 column, she went to bed at 10 p.m. and finally got out of bed in the morning at 7 a.m. That's 9 hours TIB, not counting times when she was in and out of bed throughout the night to use the bathroom or go to the couch. It is much easier to calculate SE% overall if you convert hours into minutes, so 9 hours × 60 minutes = 540 minutes. She then wrote 540 minutes in the Monday 6/24 column for the TIB row. Then calculate the TIB for each remaining night of the week using the same guidelines. Ignore the times you're technically getting out of bed to sit somewhere else or use the bathroom; instead, just use the bedtime and wake time and calculate that time span as your TIB.

Step 2. Calculate Total Sleep Time (TST). The easiest way to calculate TST is by starting with your TIB and subtracting the estimated time awake throughout the night. Take the TIB you just calculated for the first column, then subtract the time to fall asleep for the first time (in row G), total time awake after falling asleep (row I) and time between finally waking up and finally getting out of bed (time between row K and row J). This value should be in minutes; add it to the TST column for that night. Then calculate the TST for each remaining night of the week using the same guidelines.

In Ruth's example, for Monday 6/24, we have already calculated that she was in bed that night for a total of 540 minutes (10 p.m. to 7 a.m.). She recorded that it took approximately 60 minutes to fall asleep, that she was awake 15 minutes in the middle of the night, and that she woke up 15 minutes before she got out of bed. Her TST for the night, then, involves some basic subtraction: 540 minutes TIB − 60 minutes (time to fall asleep) − 15 (time awake in the middle of the night) − 15 (time between finally waking up and getting out of bed) = 450 minutes. She then put this value (450 minutes) in the TST row for the Monday 6/24 column.

It is important to note here that Ruth was generally excellent with getting right out of bed in the morning, as she was just too frustrated to stay there—most mornings she got up as soon as she awoke. If you tend to stay in bed for a while after you wake up, make sure to include all of that time in your sleep diary, since you're lying in bed awake.

Step 3. Calculate Your Sleep Efficiency Percentage (SE%) for the Night.
Take the TST you just calculated (in minutes), divide it by TIB (also in minutes), and multiply the final answer by 100. This will give you the percentage of that night that you were in bed actually asleep.

In Ruth's example, on Monday, 6/24 her TST was 450 minutes and her TIB is 540 minutes. Then we divide the two numbers and multiply by 100 to get a percentage:

$(450/540) \times 100 = 0.83 \times 100 = 83$ percent SE% for Monday night 6/24

Thus, Ruth's SE% for that night is 83 percent, suggesting that she spent about 83 percent of TIB asleep and 17 percent of TIB awake throughout that night.

Step 4. Calculate Average Total Sleep Time (TST) for the Week. Take the average across all of the nights (in minutes) for TST and divide by 7 (provided you have data for all seven nights—or just average as many nights as you recorded). In Ruth's example, at the bottom of the diary she added up each night's TST and then divided by 7 to get her TST average. Admittedly, this is not too terrible for a baseline sleep diary when you look at how much sleep she got on average, but there was definitely room for improvement to help compress her sleep more since she felt it was very broken and of poor quality.

Step 5. Calculate Your SE% Average for the Week. Take each night's SE%, add them together, and divide by 7 (assuming you have data for every night that week) to get your SE% average for the week. In Ruth's example, at the end of the week, she added up each SE% at the bottom of the diary and divided by 7 to get the average. Her SE% average was 77 percent, meaning that, on average, she was in bed and asleep 77 percent of the night across the week.

Takeaway Message: Track and Synthesize Your Sleep Data

✓ The sleep diary is a very useful tool to track your sleep patterns, synthesize your average sleep quantities, and determine how efficient you are at sleeping while in bed.

✓ Use your diary to note any obvious patterns. This will give you a great deal of insight into what you should try to change to improve your sleep

FORM 7.1: **Sleep Diary**

Fill Out Just Before Going to Bed at Night							
A. Day and date							
B. Naps							
C. Exercise							
D. Caffeine							
E. Sleep medications or alcohol							
F. Time you went to bed and turned out the lights							
Fill Out the Next Morning in Reference to the Night Before							
G. Time to fall asleep for first time							
H. Number of awakenings in middle of night							
I. Total time awake after falling asleep							
J. Time you finally woke up							
K. Time you finally got out of bed							
Your Sleep Stats: Sleep Efficiency Calculation							
Total time in bed (TIB)							
Total sleep time (TST)							
Sleep efficiency (SE%): TST/TIB × 100							

AVERAGE TST = _____

AVERAGE SE% = _____

FORM 7.2: **Ruth's Sleep Diary**

Fill Out Just Before Going to Bed at Night							
A. Day and date	Monday 6/24	Tuesday 6/25	Wednesday 6/26	Thursday 6/27	Friday 6/28	Saturday 6/29	Sunday 6/30
B. Naps	1:30–2:15	—	1–3 p.m.	—	—	2–4 p.m.	—
C. Exercise	6–6:30 p.m. walk	—	8–8:45 a.m. spin class	—	8–8:40 a.m. walk	—	12–12:45 p.m. spin class
D. Caffeine	—	Coffee: 8 oz 8 a.m., 8 oz 12 p.m.	Coffee: 8 oz 8 a.m., 8 oz 12 p.m.	Coffee: 8 oz 8 a.m., 8 oz 12 p.m.	—	Coffee: 8 oz 8 a.m., 8 oz 12 p.m.	Coffee: 8 oz 9 a.m., 8 oz 12 p.m.
E. Sleep medications or alcohol	1 glass wine 9 p.m.	—	2 glasses wine 8 p.m.	—	Zolpidem 5 mg 10 p.m.	—	1 glass wine 8 p.m.
F. Time you went to bed and turned out the lights	10 p.m.	10:45 p.m.	11:30 p.m.	8:30 p.m.	11 p.m.	11:30 p.m.	9:30 p.m.
Fill Out the Next Morning in Reference to the Night Before							
G. Time to fall asleep for first time	60 min	60 min	75 min	90 min	60 min	5 min	120 min
H. Number of awakenings in middle of night	1	4	1	2	2	1	2
I. Total time awake after falling asleep	15 min	90 min	45 min	120 min	45 min	10 min	60 min
J. Time you finally woke up	6:45 a.m.	6:45 a.m.	7:15 a.m.	7 a.m.	7 a.m.	7:30 a.m.	8:00 a.m.
K. Time you finally got out of bed	7 a.m.	6:45 a.m.	7:15 a.m.	7 a.m.	7 a.m.	7:30 a.m.	8:00 a.m.

Your Sleep Stats: Sleep Efficiency Calculation							
Total time in bed (TIB)	540 min	480 min	465 min	630 min	480 min	480 min	630 min
Total sleep time (TST)	450 min	405 min	375 min	420 min	375 min	465 min	450 min
Sleep efficiency (SE%): TST/TIB × 100	83%	69%	74%	67%	78%	97%	71%

AVERAGE TST $= 450 + 405 + 375 + 420 + 375 + 465 + 450$
$= 2940 / 7$
$= 420$ minutes (7 hours)

AVERAGE SE% $= 83\% + 69\% + 74\% + 67\% + 78\% + 97\% + 71\%$
$= 539\% / 7$ days
$= 77\%$

8.

Stomp Out the Sleep Stealers

If you're reading this book, you've probably tried sleep hygiene before, and likely with little benefit. Sleep hygiene as a standalone treatment has repeatedly been shown ineffective for chronic insomnia. Sure, some people might notice a change in their sleep by limiting coffee in the evening, but most people with chronic insomnia find that these changes don't lessen their insomnia in the long run when done alone.

So, why have a chapter dedicated solely on sleep hygiene? You can practice all the other strategies in this book to sleep better, but let's face it, if you're guzzling a 2-liter bottle of caffeinated soda in the evening, your body is likely going to have a tough time settling down for a good night despite all the other hard work you've been doing.

Proper sleep hygiene can keep your insomnia from worsening and, in the long run, can help prevent it from returning. I always think of proper sleep hygiene as the foundation on which the other treatment recommendations in this book work. For example, if you are trying to optimize your sleep drive and keep a prescribed bed and wake time, but you drink a cup of coffee at 6 p.m. every night or exercise too late in the evening, it'll be harder to wind down and become sleepy at the time you want. If your room is too noisy or bright, it might just be too hard to sleep even when you may be able to sleep when you are in a darker, quieter room.

THE BASIC SLEEP STEALERS

A number of sleep stealers—some secret, some not so secret—need attention in order to set the stage for a good night's sleep. As I said, don't expect these changes to cure your insomnia. Instead, think of them as ways to set the stage for the other treatments to do their work. If you don't have these things in order, you're likely making things more difficult in the long run—remember, short-term pain for long-term gain here.

I. Avoid Alcohol Within 3 Hours of Bedtime

You've probably had a friend say that she has a glass of wine nightly to help her sleep. Sure, that glass of wine after dinner helps you to unwind and may even make you sleepy, but it is actually doing far more damage than you might realize when it comes to sleep. The false guarantee that alcohol brings to a night of good sleep is just that—false. The problem here is that alcohol consumed close to bedtime can actually disrupt the quality and quantity of whatever sleep you might actually obtain. It isn't all about the *quantity* of sleep you get; it is also very much about the *quality*. Alcohol can help induce sleep, but then it wears off shortly afterward, leading you to awaken or have lighter sleep. Once you awaken, you might need another drink to get back to sleep, and if you start having to do that, it is a slippery slope toward your body relying on a drink to return to sleep.

This doesn't mean that you need to avoid alcohol altogether. A drink now and then, earlier in the evening, is totally fine as long as you are not relying on it as a sleep aid. And if you're out later at night at, say, a holiday party, and decide to have a drink, that's fine. Just know that it might cause you to have more disrupted sleep that night or to awaken feeling groggier than usual. Accept it, move on, and make sure to avoid alcoholic drinks before bed whenever possible.

Alcohol is a sedative that can relax the muscles in your airway. If you have any issues with snoring from time to time, or even untreated sleep apnea, alcohol can worsen them, further contributing to a night of poor-quality sleep. In addition, alcohol tends to be quite caloric, therefore putting you at a greater risk of weight gain as more and more drinks are consumed on a regular basis.

2. Limit Liquids Within 3 Hours of Bedtime

This one is pretty simple. If you drink a lot of liquids before bed, you'll be more likely to have to use the bathroom at night. A good rule of thumb is to limit your liquid intake to 1 cup maximum within 3 hours of bedtime and to always void your bladder before going to sleep.

If you have medication you need to take before bed, take a small sip of water—enough to get the medication down. Often, patients find that they are thirstier at nighttime. I find that this frequently happens because they are not drinking enough water during the daytime hours. Instead, keep a tally of how much water you drink during the day and try to get 8 cups of water in before the 3-hour cutoff before bedtime.

If you are still extremely thirsty at night, despite drinking a lot of water during the day, consider discussing this concern with your doctor, as there may be other factors that play into your excessive thirst (such as diabetes or certain medications you may be taking). Finally, if you find that dry mouth at night is causing you to drink a lot of water, suck on a few ice chips instead of drinking a whole glass of water. You'll ease your dry mouth this way but without consuming as much water. Over-the-counter products are also readily available that can help with dry mouth, including chewing gums, mouthwashes, and toothpastes.

3. No Caffeine After 2 p.m. at the Very Latest

The average cup of coffee has a half-life of 6 hours. That means that, 6 hours after it is consumed, only *half* of the caffeine has been eliminated from your body. As we get older, caffeine tends to take longer to leave the body.

Caffeine isn't found just in coffee. Many sodas, teas, chocolate, and even some over-the-counter medications (especially for migraines) can contain caffeine. A good rule of thumb is to never assume that coffee, soda, or tea is decaffeinated. Make sure it clearly says "decaffeinated" on the label. And just because it is diet soda doesn't necessarily mean that it is decaffeinated either. "Diet" means fewer calories, not less caffeine.

Caffeine doesn't just make it harder to fall asleep; it can also cause disrupted or shallow sleep throughout the night. If you need a pick-me-up in the afternoon, consider taking a short walk in the sunlight or eating your lunch near a bright window to perk up naturally. Exercise and sunlight can be just as alerting as a cup of coffee.

4. Keep Your Bedroom Cool

Many people like to create a cocoon-like environment for sleep. But while it might feel nice to be warm and cozy at night, a room that's too warm (or even one that's too cold) can cause multiple awakenings at night, thereby leading to disrupted and poor-quality sleep. A few hours before the body goes to sleep every night, there is a very subtle drop in body temperature to help prepare for sleep. Then, throughout the night, the body's temperature continues to drop ever so slightly until 2 hours before wake time, when it starts to warm up again. Sleeping in a bedroom that's too warm makes it harder for the body to naturally drop in temperature.

The ideal temperature for sleep varies somewhat from person to person, but, somewhat surprisingly to many, a temperature in the range of 65–67 degrees Fahrenheit is often ideal. All too often, I hear my women patients complain about having a different internal thermostat from their bed partner, with one liking the room hot and the other wanting it cold. A simple fix for this is to keep the room cooler overall, but then put two separate comforters on the bed that have different weights/

thicknesses. This way, you're sleeping in the same bed as your spouse, but you don't have to share one comforter that might not be ideal for your internal thermostat. If you have a radiator that's hard to control, consider opening your window before you go to sleep—even in the winter—and leave it open a crack throughout the night. Your best bet is to keep your bedroom cool and have multiple blankets on the bed to put on and take off as needed.

5. Keep Your Bedroom Dark

Our bodies are meant to sleep when it is dark and awaken when the sun comes up. We need darkness to induce sleep and keep us asleep. Remember, melatonin (aka the "hormone of darkness") needs darkness to work its magic—not just dim light, but darkness. We can sense even the tiniest bit of light through our eyelids when they are closed, and that will send a signal to your brain that the sun is out and we should start to wake up. Even if you don't think that the early morning sun or the street lamp outside can impact your sleep, it likely does.

The best way to limit light in your room is to purchase light-blocking shades. Simply having shades on your windows is not enough—room-darkening shades are great, but they're not light blocking. In my bedroom as well as both of my children's rooms, I have light-blocking roman shades on the windows. Since they're set inside the window frame, I have heavy floor-length light-blocking drapes framing each window to also limit any light streaming through the sides of the roman shades. Many hotels have it just right with their light-blocking window treatments, so get a cue from them and notice what they've done.

You need not spend a lot of money on window treatments, as many online discount stores sell them relatively inexpensively. I even made inexpensive light-blocking drapes for my daughter's room using a DIY website's instructions, light-blocking liner fabric, no-sew tape, and curtain ring clips (sewing is not my strength). And although it might not be the most attractive of options, a simple black garbage bag can do the trick when taped over the window. Finally, if you aren't bothered by sleeping with a sleep mask, this is another easy option to block the light if you aren't able to make all the changes to your window treatments.

Also take note of any electronics in your room that may be emitting even the faintest of light. Some cable boxes, phones, and computers can brighten your room, so try to tape over them, turn them off, or just remove them from your room altogether.

6. Keep Your Bedroom Quiet

Noise, especially irregular noise, is a frequent disruptor of sleep and can even worsen the quality of sleep one gets at night. Evaluate your room for any noises that might be an issue and try to remedy them. The ideal situation is to get thicker windows and drywall, and if you have the means and time to do so, by all means go ahead. However, for many people, it isn't an option, so the next best thing to do is get earplugs (look for the silicone earplugs for swimmers) and/or a white noise machine. There are many different types of machines on the market; try to look for ones that emit constant sounds and ideally straight white noise. Many smartphones now have white noise apps you can download so you do not always need to take your machine with you when you travel. Whenever I travel, I ask for a room far from the elevator and ideally on a higher floor. I have even stayed at a hotel that provided white noise machines in each room—no harm in asking if they have them!

I frequently hear about patients who have bed partners who snore at night, and that it disrupts their sleep, often making it impossible to fall asleep. The first thing to do is make sure that your bed partner does not a sleep problem, such as sleep apnea. Are there any pauses in breathing at night? Is there any choking or gasping in addition to snoring? Is the snoring loud? If the answer to any of these questions is yes, you might want to consider having an honest discussion with your bed partner about how you are concerned with long-term health and to consider an evaluation. This may help with the snoring and any other disruptive nighttime behaviors. If your partner is evaluated and nothing can be done, you might want to consider some ways to block the noise, including a white noise machine or ear plugs. Sometimes, the best—and last—solution is to just sleep in separate beds or bedrooms. It lessens the pressure to sleep well, reduces frustrations and tensions in the relationship, and allows for healthier sleep and communication overall. Sure, go to one bed at the beginning of the night and have sex and cuddle for a little while if you'd like—but at lights out, retire to your own beds for a night of quiet, undisturbed sleep.

I also frequently work with women who are in the role of caretaker in the house, whether taking care of children or elderly relatives. Blocking the noise in this case may not be advisable as it is necessary to hear anyone who might need you in the middle of the night. This situation does set one up for a poor night's sleep at times because you are always, in essence, waiting for someone call your name. Whenever possible, practice acceptance that there is not much you can do that night and try to get others to help on some nights as well, to relieve you from your duties for at least a chunk of time and allow for a better night of sleep.

7. Take a Warm Bath (at the Proper Time)

As mentioned just before, good sleepers tend to have a slight drop in their body temperature just as sleep begins each night. Poor sleepers, however, don't have as much of a drop. So while taking a warm shower or bath just before bedtime sounds like a good idea to relax and unwind from the stressors of the day, it can actually warm up your body temperature even more, thereby impacting your natural ability to fall asleep. The key here is timing: it's best to take a warm shower or bath 1.5–2 hours before bedtime, which can facilitate the cooling-off process the body is meant to experience before sleep. A 20-minute warm bath (not scalding, just warm—no need to make yourself uncomfortable here) 1.5–2 hours before bedtime can help induce sleepiness in patients with insomnia. Make sure to talk with your doctor before you start taking warm showers and baths, as some medical conditions may be worsened from them.

Although most of the research was done using actual baths (Liao, 2002), it can also work if you take a shower. However, if you have the time, why not indulge in a quiet, dimly lit bubble bath with a good book for 20 minutes? Further, although no empirical data support this, I have had a handful of menopausal patients over the years who swore by hot baths as a way to help with hot flashes at night. They all reported that they noticed a sharp increase in nighttime hot flashes on the nights that they did not take a hot bath.

Taking a shower in the morning is fine if you regularly do this, but it won't help or hurt your sleep at night. On the other hand, taking a hot shower just before bed (within 1 hour of bedtime) can actually warm you up too much, making it harder for your body to naturally become sleepy. Remember, the key here is to warm your body up but then have it cool off that hour before bed, to signal that the body is ready for sleep. As a side note, a study suggested that wearing socks to bed helps with passive body heating as well and improves sleep (Ko & Lee 2018). More research is definitely needed in this area, but there's no harm in trying out some of your socks in bed at night!

8. Exercise 4–6 Hours Before Bedtime

Exercise can deepen sleep. Increasing deeper sleep can make you less vulnerable to things that can wake up you (such as pain, noise, or hot flashes). As discussed earlier, good sleepers tend to have their core body temperature begin to cool off just before bed, drop throughout the night, and warm up again a few hours before waking up. Exercise (even 20 minutes of light aerobic exercise) done anywhere between 4 and 6 hours before bedtime can help warm up the body initially and then cool off during the time just before bed, mimicking what happens with good sleepers. Occasionally, patients with insomnia may work out right before bed in an attempt to "tire" themselves out. While this may make your body tired, it does not typically induce sleepiness, as it warms up the body at bedtime, making it harder to fall asleep.

Find an exercise that works for you and make it as fun as possible. If you are at home and unable to get outside or to a gym, there are many free 20-minute exercise videos on the Internet (such as YouTube) that can range from guided walking to high-intensity interval training, yoga, or Pilates. There are even modified exercise programs available online if you have any physical limitations (such as chair yoga videos). Always make sure to check with your doctor first before beginning any new exercise regimen. Also, if you find that you don't have enough time to exercise regularly, you can try the warm bath technique some evenings (remember, 1.5–2 hours before bed) on the days you are unable to exercise in the early evening.

9. Time Your Meals Properly

Heavy, large, or spicy meals within 3 hours of bedtime can wreak havoc on your sleep. When you go to bed at night, your body needs to be shutting down from the day as well. By giving it a large meal to digest instead, you're making the process of shutting down more difficult. In addition, heavy, creamy, or acidic meals can worsen acid reflux, making your sleep more restless and leading to more awakenings. Finally, as with alcohol, the extra calories at night only make it harder to metabolize the meal and can lead to weight gain, increasing your risk of snoring or even sleep apnea. The flip side of the coin here, though, is that going to bed without any food can make you wake up hungry or even with a case of low blood sugar. A small snack just before bedtime can remedy this, and a combination of a carbohydrate with a small amount of protein (such as half a banana with a tablespoon of peanut butter, or a whole wheat cracker with a slice of cheese) can help promote sleepiness.

10. Avoid Nicotine, Especially Within 3 Hours of Bedtime

Nicotine is a stimulant. Although it might be calming to you to have that cigarette when you want to wind down, it is actually waking you up. Even worse, if you tend to smoke in the middle of the night, you are likely waking up because of nicotine withdrawal. Smoking when you wake up helps further the addiction to nicotine, as well as creating a learned behavioral pattern to wake up repeatedly at night. It is ideal to stop smoking overall, both for your health and for your sleep at night. However, if total smoking cessation at once is overwhelming, consider limiting your nicotine in the middle of the night. Once you stop smoking in the middle of the night, then you can work on cutting down the cigarettes before bed, with your last cigarette 3 hours before bedtime.

11. Make Friends With Your Alarm Clock . . . Seven Days a Week

It can be very tempting to not set the alarm on the mornings you do not need to wake up for anything in particular. However, any time you sleep later than your prescribed, routine wake-up time, you put yourself at risk for having sleep troubles either the next night or the night afterward. Sleeping even an hour later than you should in the morning reduces the time you are awake for the day, thus reducing your "sleep hunger" and making it harder to fall asleep or stay asleep on subsequent nights. Regardless of how much sleep you obtained the night before, always get up to your alarm clock. And don't hit the snooze button either—whatever sleep you get after you hit it will only be unrefreshing and broken. It isn't worth the cost in the long run: more insomnia—remember, short-term pain for long-term gain. Consistency with your bedtime and, even more important, your wake time is crucial to obtaining a solid night of sleep in the long run. It works for many people.

On the other hand, if you're someone who is always wide awake hours before you need to get up, still make sure to set your alarm clock. Although you may think it'll never happen, you'll never need it, don't leave it to chance. There could be that one random morning where you actually are able to sleep later than the time you need to awaken. Although it might feel nice to allow that to happen, don't let it. Set the alarm every morning—even if you don't think you need it. It'll pay off in the long run.

12. Block the Blue Light

As noted earlier, melatonin is the hormone of darkness. It is regulated by our circadian rhythm and comes out naturally in our brains 1–2 hours before bedtime, helping to induce sleepiness. Melatonin levels drop when we are exposed to light, and this is especially true with blue light. Sunlight contains many different spectrums of light, including red, orange, yellow, green, and blue light rays. When combined, they make "white light"—also known as sunlight. Blue light, on the other hand, is primarily short-wavelength light (not as full spectrum as white light) and is typically emitted from most electronics, including tablets, phones, computers, and televisions. Melatonin doesn't love light to begin with, but it really doesn't like short-wavelength blue light. Simply put, using electronics at night drops your melatonin levels, thereby making you less sleepy. Chang et al. (2015) looked at this issue in-depth and examined the effects of reading on a blue-light device compared with an "old-fashioned" printed book. The participants who read on tablets took longer to fall asleep, were more awake before bedtime, took longer to wake up in the morning, and had less REM sleep at night (active sleep, when we process emotions, learn, consolidate memories, and dream the most).

It is best to limit all blue light exposure within 1–2 hours (ideally 2 hours) before your bedtime and to not use any electronics throughout the night when you wake up or cannot sleep. Read a book or a magazine, practice mindfulness meditation, scrapbook—find something that works for you that is quiet, calm, and relaxing and does not rely on blue light. Do not sit in the dark at night; just turn on a dim lamp with a white light bulb. Sitting in the dark will only make you focus more on being awake and not being sleepy.

If you find it very difficult to relax without the use of electronics, there are various ways to help block the blue light. Blue-blocking glasses are readily available at online retailers such as amazon.com. You can also look into downloading apps for your computer (such as f.lux) that can put a filter on your computer to block blue light. Finally, many phones now have a nighttime feature that will create a reddish hue, helping limit blue light exposure at night. Although there is quite a bit of debate about just how effective all of these blue-blocking technologies can be, some people find them very helpful, and if it at least makes you somewhat more mindful about your nighttime behaviors and electronic usage, I am all in favor of making small steps towards ultimately going tech-free at night. All that being said, you should still consider the content of what you are reading on a tablet or your phone. Often, we are reading the latest news (which isn't often that pleasant or calming in today's society), work e-mails, or social media posts. The content of these media may create more anxiety or stress, making it harder to fall asleep as well.

Consider whether cutting down on electronic use may be another goal for you if you really struggle with putting down your phone or tablet at night. A good way of limiting your electronic use at night is to have a space outside of your bedroom (such as a box in the kitchen) where you keep all household tablets and phones with their chargers. Before wind-down time, or at the very least before retiring to bed, put your phone and tablet in the box and charge them overnight.

13. Wind Down One Hour Before Bed

Sleep is not an on/off switch. Instead, we need to treat it like a dimmer switch. Set the stage for sleep beginning 1 hour before bed and find relaxing rituals that you can do every night to help prepare your body for sleep. Wind-down activities vary from person to person, though many people enjoy reading a book or magazine, engaging in a quiet hobby, or doing gentle nighttime yoga stretches or a mindfulness meditation exercise that may incorporate deep breathing or muscle relaxation. Find what works for you—ideally without relying on blue-light-emitting electronics. If there's some music or a relaxation exercise on your phone that you like to listen to, just turn it on but then immediately turn the phone over (or use a blue light filter app as mentioned earlier). If you struggle to find a full hour to wind down, try to aim for at least 30 minutes.

14. Don't Watch the Clock

Clock watching does not make the night pass any faster or slower, and it does not help you to fall asleep. Instead, checking the clock to see how long you've been awake or how long you have until you need to get up for the morning only makes you more tense, anxious, and stressed. Get an old-fashioned alarm clock (so you don't have to rely on a cell phone or tablet to wake you up) and put it under your bed. Make sure to tape over or turn around any clocks in your room to help remove the temptation to look at night. Clock watching can be a difficult habit to break at first, as it sometimes gives people a false sense of control over the night. In reality, it doesn't help you sleep any better. Look at the clock just before getting into bed and don't look at it again until the alarm clock goes off again in the morning.

15. Avoid Naps

Staying awake during the day will help you fall asleep faster at night. Many people with insomnia often can't nap even when they try, but some people do struggle with this issue. You may also feel more of an urge to nap as you change your sleep patterns during treatment for insomnia. If you begin to feel excessively sleepy during the day and struggle with staying awake, a 20-minute nap before 2 p.m. is advisable. Ideally, take a nap in your bed whenever possible, and set the alarm for 30 minutes to allow for some time to fall asleep. Longer naps and naps later in the day can interfere more with your nighttime sleep. If you still have significant issues with sleepiness during treatment, ones that are not alleviated by a nap, consider talking with your doctor regarding this issue.

ADDITIONAL STRATEGIES DURING PREGNANCY

Pregnancy can be a time of great discomfort that can lead to sleep disruption. There are a few things you can do to help deal with this as best as possible and minimize the effects of discomfort on your sleep. In addition to the above-mentioned strategies that are applicable to all women, here's some strategies many pregnant women find particularly helpful.

1. Sleep on Your Left Side

Many women who start out as stomach sleepers worry that they cannot sleep on their stomach during the first trimester. While it likely won't do any harm to the baby at the very beginning of your pregnancy, when you're not showing at all, it will quickly become uncomfortable to sleep in that position as your belly grows. Stomach sleeping is not advised once you are showing.

Back sleeping is also not recommended. During the second trimester, the uterus becomes large enough to impact blood flow whenever you sleep on your back. The inferior vena cava and aorta both become compressed, and the main blood supply is reduced to both your body and placenta. As a result of this decreased blood supply to the heart, pregnant moms occasionally may awaken with a racing heart or shortness of breath.

Side sleeping is ideal, especially your *left side*, as it improves circulation and alleviates pressure to the inferior vena cava. If you're not someone who usually is a side sleeper, get into this habit early on in pregnancy. It is most comfortable to sleep on your side with knees bent.

Please *do not* obsess about your sleeping position if you happen to move throughout the night (as we all do!). When you wake up, just move back to the side position. Your body has a natural mechanism built in to wake you up when you're uncomfortable. Just accept it, move back to your left side, and go back to sleep. Worrying about it will only lead to less sleep.

2. Pillows Are Your Best Friend

A pregnancy pillow or wedge pillow can be a fantastic way to support your back, belly, and legs. Experiment with extra pillows to support your back and help you not roll onto your back in the middle of the night. Placing a pillow between your legs can support your lower back, and a full body pregnancy or wedge pillow under your belly can help reduce pressure in your abdomen. If you continue to roll onto your back during pregnancy and are continually worried about it, consider wearing a large pocket T-shirt backward and sew a tennis ball into the pocket. If you roll onto your back, you'll be uncomfortable and roll back onto your side.

If, despite trying over and over, you still can't comfortably make the switch to your side, use pillows to prop yourself into an incline. Sleeping on your back at a 45-degree tilt can prevent a lot of the compression. Talk with your obstetrician first to make sure that this propped up position is OK, as the standard recommendation is to avoid back sleeping.

3. Focus on Eating and Liquids

Especially when you are pregnant, be extra vigilant about your food and liquid intake. Heartburn can be a major issue for many women during pregnancy, so limit foods that might trigger this (acidic foods, chocolate, coffee, fatty and rich foods). Simply eating too close to bedtime can cause or worsen heartburn as well, and sleeping propped up can help alleviate some of the symptoms. If heartburn is severe enough despite these changes, medication options are available—talk with your doctor regarding what is safe to take during pregnancy.

Nausea can also awaken women in the middle of the night. Bland snacks such as saltines can help settle the stomach. Others find that ginger is helpful, too. Ginger ale can be helpful for nausea, but be careful of additional liquid intake in the middle of the night as it can increase awakenings to urinate.

4. Naps(?)

Naps aren't ideal overall, but sometimes there's an overwhelming sense of sleepiness and fatigue during pregnancy, especially during the first trimester. If this is the case, a nap may be advisable to get through the day. Try, as best as possible, to limit the nap to 20 minutes and before 2 p.m. Also, when possible, nap only in your bed to help teach your body to sleep only in your bed.

5. Exercise

Exercise is especially helpful during pregnancy. Prenatal yoga is a great way to strengthen the body and calm the mind. Make sure to get the OK from your obstetrician before you start any exercise regimen.

ADDITIONAL STRATEGIES DURING PERIMENOPAUSE

Hot flashes and night sweats tend to be the biggest issue for most women during the transition to menopause. Here are a few sleep hygiene strategies that might help.

I. Keep the Bedroom Cool

Make friends with the floor/desk fan, air conditioner, or ceiling fan. A cool room is ideal throughout the night.

2. Bedside Cold Compress

Keep a bowl of ice next to your bed with a washcloth on top of it. When you wake up in the middle of the night with a hot flash, put the ice-cold washcloth on the back of your neck. This helps to cool you down fast.

3. Dress in Light, Moisture-Wicking Pajamas

Night sweats lead to moisture-drenched pajamas that can make you shiver and have trouble returning to sleep without changing your clothing. Although a middle-of-the-night pajamas change is often warranted, moisture-wicking pajamas (made from lightweight polyester fabrics, similar to what is used in athletic gear) are easily available online and may decrease sleep disturbance.

4. Separate Bedding

Although it may not be as pretty, consider having your bed made in many layers that can be taken off throughout the night. If your bed partner finds this problematic, consider using several smaller comforters—some for your side of the bed and others for your bed partner's.

Takeaway Message: Sleep Hygiene

- ✓ Sleep hygiene alone is not usually a cure for insomnia, but it helps act as a foundation for the other treatment modules in this book.
- ✓ Remember to limit liquids, heavy meals, alcohol, and nicotine within 3 hours of bedtime and to wind down without blue light 1 hour before bedtime.
- ✓ Avoid naps and caffeine after 2 p.m., and get up at the same time every single morning.
- ✓ Practicing good sleep hygiene will put you well on your way to effectively adding in the other treatment modules described in the following chapters.

9.

Learn to Love Your Bed Again

OK, ladies, it's time for a pop quiz: when you think of your bed, what are the first three things you think of? Write them down here:

1. _____
2. _____
3. _____

How was this exercise? Was it easy? Challenging? Stupid? How long did it take you to come up with the answers?

More times than not, patients with insomnia don't answer this question immediately, or easily. I have posed this question to hundreds of women with insomnia, and most of them say that the bed is about rest, tossing and turning, or frustration. If your first answer above is "sleep," then congrats! You passed the test with flying colors. If you wrote something other than sleep (even "rest"), then you have a lot of room for improvement and are by far in the majority when it comes to women with insomnia. How can you expect yourself to sleep in your bed if you don't even immediately associate it with sleep?

Many people took some form of a Psych 101 class in college or even high school. If you did, you probably learned about a scientist named Ivan Pavlov and his discovery of classical conditioning. Pavlov was busy doing experiments with dogs and noticed that whenever he put meat powder in front of a dog, the dog would salivate. Makes sense, right? If you put an ice cream sundae in front of me, I'd probably salivate, too! Pavlov then tried ringing a bell whenever the meat powder was presented to the dogs. Meat powder = salivate, but because the bell was introduced at the same time as the meat powder, the bell became associated with meat powder as well. Then either the bell *or* the meat powder would cause them to salivate. By pairing meat powder with ringing the bell, Pavlov conditioned the dogs to salivate on hearing the once-neutral bell, even without the meat powder present.

So you might be thinking, *What does a salivating dog have to do with me tossing and turning at night?* Good question. Let's take Emily, for example, a 43-year-old divorced business executive. Emily began suffering from insomnia 6 years earlier when she started having relationship difficulties coupled with multiple work stressors. What initially began as some mild trouble with falling asleep gradually turned into a 1- to 2-hour delay in falling asleep, coupled with awakening an hour before her alarm clock. Whenever she was unable to sleep, she would get up to use the bathroom once and would get back in bed with the hope that sleep would eventually come. She would then toss and turn for hours, watching the clock and worrying about anything and everything in her life (including what would happen the next day if she couldn't sleep). If it was a night when she wasn't particularly worried about anything, she would then lay in bed as still as possible, listening to meditation apps in an attempt to force sleep to happen. When she woke up in the early morning, she would check the clock and again lay as still as possible for a short while. If that didn't work, she would then turn on the television and lay there until her alarm clock went off.

Before she developed insomnia, she had an occasional bad night now and then, but nothing of concern. In fact, when she found that she wasn't tired or sleepy in the past, she typically wasn't bothered by it and instead saw it as a time to do work in her office or get things done around the house. When she was finally sleepy and decided to go to bed for the night, she would get in bed, turn out the lights, and fall asleep within 20 minutes (often even quicker). She would wake up once at night, use the bathroom, and then go right back to sleep, only to wake up within 10 minutes of her alarm going off in the morning. Before she developed insomnia, Emily didn't give much thought to sleep and didn't put a lot of effort into getting to sleep. I gave her the same pop quiz I gave you at the beginning of this chapter, and her answers were "rest, frustration, and (finally) sleep."

When Emily came to my office, she was most frustrated with the fact that she would come home from work by 8 p.m. every night, eat dinner, and then sit on the couch to watch reality television, struggling to keep her eyes open. She was constantly fighting sleep whenever she was on the couch, which constantly gave her the false confidence that "I'm so sleepy right now, tonight will *definitely* be the night I'll go to sleep!" Once she was struggling to stay awake, she would then get up and go to bed. Each time she got into bed, her mind would then completely wake up, and she was back to tossing and turning in bed, having lost the sleepiness she had on the couch. Night after night, she would come close to falling asleep on the couch, only to then wake up when she got in bed.

So why did the bed become associated with frustration when it used to be a relaxing place for sleep? The reason is based on classical conditioning theory—that's right, the same theory involving Pavlov's dogs. When good sleepers go to sleep at night, their brains say *bed = sleep*. Essentially, the bed is "paired"—to use classical conditioning language—with sleep. Whenever a good sleeper gets in bed, an automatic signal is sent to the brain that says it's time to go to sleep. Once insomnia starts, however, more time is spent lying in bed awake, tossing and turning, worrying, being frustrated, watching TV, or using computers or phones. After a few weeks of introducing these other behaviors into the bed during times when you're supposed to be asleep, the pairing of bed = sleep begins to weaken and the bed now becomes paired strongly with whatever awake behaviors are being done in bed. So now, instead of signaling sleep, the bed signals awake.

As in Emily's case, the most powerful example of this occurs whenever I hear patients say they are so sleepy on the couch watching TV at night, but when they get into bed shortly afterward, the sleepiness is gone and they are wide awake in bed with an alert brain. Again, the bed is now paired—whether you like it or not!—with being awake. The more time you spend in bed lying awake with insomnia, the worse the insomnia gets.

So how do you fix this association problem? Stimulus control is the answer. One of the oldest insomnia treatment recommendations, stimulus control was developed by Richard Bootzin, Ph.D., in the 1970s. It has lots of research support behind it and is considered a standard treatment for chronic insomnia. Stimulus control refers to controlling the use of the stimulus—in this case, using the bed for sleep only.

Stimulus control is really simple in theory but difficult in practice unless you are really committed and truly understand that a negative association is created between the bed and being awake instead of a positive association between the bed and sleep. The bed is *solely* for sleep and sex—that's it.

STIMULUS CONTROL: THE BASIC RULES

I've said this several times throughout the book, but I cannot stress it enough. Consistency is key. You're retraining your body clock and, here, your brain. If you occasionally break the stimulus control rules, you're giving a confusing signal to your brain and body. Even though we are smart humans who rationally understand that the bed *should* be associated only with sleep, we are still animals. As a result, we still respond to conditioning theory just as any animal does.

1. Go to Bed Only When You're Sleepy, but Not Before the Set Bedtime

Chapter 10 discusses setting your optimal bedtime. This bedtime will likely change (ideally moving earlier) as treatment progresses, but for the sake of this rule, try to not go to bed before the set bedtime each week. You can always go to bed later than your set bedtime if you're not sleepy, but try not to get in bed earlier even if you are tired or sleepy—remember, short-term pain for long-term gain. It won't be easy at first, but ideally it will get easier as your sleep improves.

Sleepiness is not the same as fatigue. People with insomnia typically feel fatigued most of the time—a feeling of no energy, feeling exhausted both in mind and body. However, when you're tired, you're not always sleepy. I often hear patients say, "I am so tired but I just can't nap even when I really try." This is because fatigue and sleepiness are not the same thing. If you're sleepy, your body is able to nap. Chances are, if you have trouble going to sleep at the beginning of the night, you're likely getting in bed due to fatigue, but your body is not sufficiently sleepy. Sleepiness involves some or all of these feelings: a need to doze, head nodding, yawning, eye rubbing, a heaviness in your limbs, eyes blurring or tearing, or losing focus, attention, or concentration while reading or engaging in a relaxing/mundane task at night. See Form 9.1 to help evaluate whether you are sleepy or fatigued (or both!).

Sleepiness is key here when it comes to following Rule #1. for stimulus control. Go to bed only when you're sleepy, not when you're solely fatigued. Make sure to always check in with yourself at night as to whether you're sleepy or fatigued. If your set bedtime comes and you're not yet sleepy, just continue to stay awake doing your wind-down routine. Once sleepiness comes, you're welcome to get into bed.

2. The Bed Is Only for Sleep—Sex Is the Only Exception

Remember, the crux of stimulus control is about reassociating your bed with sleep. Sex is the only exception. If you're doing something and you aren't sure if it is within the rules, ask yourself, *Am I asleep? Am I having sex?* If the answer to both those questions is no, then out of the bed you must go. That means no TV, computer, phone, eating, lengthy conversations, tablets, books, music, or lengthy tossing and turning in bed. Go old school and get an alarm clock to put across from your bed (turned around so you don't look at it) to remove any temptation to look at your phone if you use it as an alarm clock. I've had many discussions with women over the years about their need to wind down in bed with a good book before going to sleep. The point of this exercise is about conditioning and retraining your brain that the bed is for *sleep* activities—not restful, quiet, enjoyable awake ones. Consider trying to go to bed when you're sleepy by reading outside of bed first. If you find that you're very much against this, start by limiting the amount of time you read in bed to 15 minutes maximum. Then decrease the amount of time every few nights until you are not relying on something else in the bed and can pair the bed only with sleep. I'm all in favor of you reading just before bed to wind down, just ideally not *in* your bed! If you don't even want to try to cut out reading in bed at this point, simply consider how well it has worked as a strategy in fixing your sleep problems.

3. Get Out of Bed If You Can't Sleep

Give yourself a little time to fall asleep,; approximately 20 minutes is good. Don't watch the clock, though. Clock watching throughout the night is sleep's enemy. Most people watch the clock to try to gain a sense of control over the night, thinking, *I have X many hours until I have to wake up, I really must sleep.* This leads to increased anxiety, muscle tension, and pressure to sleep—all things that erase just what you're trying to obtain.

When you're lying in bed and realize you haven't fallen asleep yet and are getting frustrated or having very active thought processes, that's the sign it has been about 20 minutes and it is time to get out of bed.

If you're lying in bed, awake and unable to sleep, get up and go somewhere else—ideally, outside the bedroom. If you're in a studio apartment and there's truly nowhere else to go, get out of your bed and sit in a chair instead. If you suffer from issues with dizziness, stability when getting out of bed, or neuropathy and are extremely hesitant to get out of bed, at least sit up in bed to make a demarcation between sitting up in bed for awake and laying down in bed for sleep.

Don't just sit there, staring in the dark and waiting for sleepiness to come. You'll just get more frustrated. Instead, find something to do that's quiet, calm, and relaxing—and in dim light—that passes the time. The activity you choose is a very personal one as one activity might be too alerting for one person and very calming for another. You might require a bit of trial-and-error here. Many of my patients have chosen to do light house work (dusting, dishes, folding laundry), jigsaw puzzles, easy cross-word puzzles or sudoku (ones that won't keep you up waiting to find the answer!), reading (magazines and short stories tend to be best because you can put them down), knitting, scrapbooking, or deep breathing, muscle relaxation, or mindfulness exercises.

When you get up and out of bed, make sure not to use anything with screens (such as computers, tablets, TV, phones). These devices emit blue light that then sends a signal to your brain that the sun is still out, suppressing melatonin. Remember, melatonin (produced naturally in our brains) is the hormone of darkness, and it especially dislikes blue light. If you have a specific relaxation app that you like to use, or a podcast or music that you enjoy listening to for a calming nighttime activity, see if you can set your tablet on "nighttime mode" to block blue light. You can also easily purchase blue-blocking goggles online. Finally, if you really must, just turn on the electronic device but then turn it over so you just listen to the app but aren't looking at the screen.

Stay outside of the bed area, engaging in your quiet activity, for as long as it takes for your body to give you signals that it is sleepy. Don't try to force sleepiness to happen; you need to trust that sleepiness comes in waves throughout the night, and you might have to wait until another wave comes over you. The more you try to force sleepiness, the more it won't happen.

4. Don't Return to Bed Until You're Sleepy

When you start to get the above-mentioned signals that you're sleepy, get back in bed. If sleep comes, great! If it doesn't, give yourself about 20 minutes (remember, don't watch the clock—just estimate!). If you haven't fallen asleep during those 20 minutes, get up and repeat Step #3 again. The bed is only for sleep and sex; laying there, tossing and turning, and trying to force sleep to happen again will only weaken that association and make it harder to sleep in the future. Consistency works with this rule, so if you're awake in bed and can't fall asleep, just get up and go engage in calming activities.

There might even be an occasional night or two when you're just sitting up outside the bed and never get to sleep that night. It may happen, but the more you get back in bed and just lie there, the more you weaken the association between bed and sleep. Stick with it! Stimulus control is extremely effective for many patients who suffer from chronic insomnia.

5. Get Out of Bed When Your Alarm Clock Goes Off

As with keeping a consistent bedtime, a consistent wake time (7 days a week!) is crucial to obtaining a solid night's sleep on a regular basis. This means that you must set your alarm clock for the same time, every day. Give yourself 5 minutes, and then get up and start your day. Laying in bed in the morning only leads to association with laying there, resting, or even getting little bits of sleep here and there that is not really refreshing. Instead, wake up, get out of your bed, and start your day. You'll eventually find that this becomes easier as it becomes an automatic habit. Also, get up at that set time every morning, *regardless of how much sleep you go the night before*—remember, short-term pain for long-term gain. Chapter 10 goes into greater detail on how to set an ideal bed and wake schedule to compress your sleep throughout the night.

TROUBLESHOOTING: THE KEY TO MASTERING STIMULUS CONTROL

The rational part of your brain is essentially asleep late at night, and you might find that talking yourself into doing stimulus control at 3 a.m. might be extremely challenging (recall the "commonsense" perpetuating factors mentioned in Chapter 3). Although the basic stimulus control instructions are quite simple—bed is only for sleep, get up if you can't sleep, and get in bed again only if you're sleepy—the most gains are made here when you're proactive and troubleshoot potential issues that might get in the way. Think ahead of time what obstacles you might encounter in following stimulus control, and figure out how you can make following stimulus control at night almost seamless, limiting as much as possible how much thought you have to put into it late at night.

Ideally, if you follow the guidelines set out in this book, including stimulus control, most nights you will get in bed and sleep through the night with minimal time awake until you get up in the morning. With that improvement, in the long run, you won't have much time awake in bed or need to get up and engage in stimulus control!

In the meantime, consider how to solve problems you might encounter in following stimulus control, ahead of time as much as you can. Here's a list of the most common problems that my patients have faced over the years, with some suggestions to overcome them and keep you on track.

Problem 1: There's Nothing to Do in the Middle of the Night—Everyone Is Asleep Except Me

Yes, it can feel quite lonely when you're awake at, say, 3 a.m. and your family is fast asleep. Instead of tricking yourself into thinking that there's nothing to do and it is just easier to lay in bed and wait for sleep to come again, come up with a list of the various things that you can do in the middle of the night. Make it easy for yourself, without the need to think about what to do. If it is cold out, have slippers and a robe right next to your bed so you can put them right on and head to the couch with a nice, cozy blanket waiting for you by a dimly lit lamp. Don't just sit in the dark, staring and hoping to fall asleep on the couch. That will only make you focus more on your sleep, making it harder to relax. Also, if you try to sleep on the couch, you're teaching yourself to sleep on the couch, not in your bed. Have a stack of magazines, easy crossword puzzles, scrapbooks, knitting, books (whatever you find calm, quiet, and relaxing) all in a basket next to the couch. That way, everything is there for you to do when you need to get up, and you don't need to make any decisions.

Problem 2: What If I Never Get Sleepy? I Might Lose That Sleepiness If I Get Up

It is very possible that you might have a night where you just aren't sleepy. This can happen from time to time for some people. You may have also had tiny episodes of sleep throughout the night (we call them *microsleep episodes* in the sleep field) that you're not even aware of. Just laying in bed resting is only doing more harm, so if you're not feeling sleepy, just get up and relax on the couch (but don't sleep there!). Rest on the couch is no different than rest in the bed, except that rest on the couch helps to reassociate the bed for *sleep only*. It can be extremely frustrating if you don't sleep at all and you may have lots of anxiety about how you'll perform the next day. Part 3 of this book offers other ways to challenge your worries/concerns about lack of sleep and its effect on you during the day and night.

If you are worried that any sleepiness you have will disappear when you get out of bed and you'll be too alert, know that sleep comes in waves. You may indeed wake up a bit by getting out of bed, but if you sit outside the bed area and engage in something quiet, calm, and relaxing in dim light, another wave of sleepiness will likely come over you, and you can return to bed at that time.

Problem 3: I Don't Want to Get Out of Bed Because I Think I'm Going to Fall Asleep in a Few Minutes

The rational side of your brain typically isn't functioning at its peak at night. Instead of continuing to stay in bed, waiting for the sleepiness to actually *put* you to sleep, I suggest you play the "one chance rule." If you are awake and know you should get up, but think you might be sleepy and may even fall asleep soon, and don't want to get out of bed, give yourself 10 minutes—the "one chance" to fall back asleep. Don't look at the clock, just estimate. If it has been around 10 minutes and you're still awake, you fooled yourself into trying to stay in bed longer. You gave yourself one chance and it didn't work, so get up and follow the stimulus control rules.

Problem 4: I Need to Know the Time at Night

Knowing what time it is at night doesn't do you any good. Instead, it creates tension as you're doing math to figure out how many hours you have left until you have to get up. And that process doesn't help to make you sleepy, it only makes you stay up more. Set your alarm clock in the morning, and then turn it around or put it under the bed. Tape over any other clocks in your room or on your walk to where you will sit if you get up to do stimulus control, to help prevent you from looking at the time when you're sitting outside the bed area. Again, do something quiet, calm, and relaxing to help pass the time so you aren't focused on the time.

Problem 5: I Don't Want to Wake Up My Bed Partner

Before you get started in stimulus control, have a talk with your bed partner about why you're going to follow these rules and how you hope it will help you in the long run. Explain that this is something that, over time, is meant to reduce the amount of time you'll be awake at night, so this will not likely be long term. If you need to, consider getting earplugs or a white noise machine for your partner to help reduce noise when you get out of bed at night.

Problem 6: If I Get Up Just a Few Hours Earlier Than My Usual Wake Time, I Might as Well Just Start My Day

You may hear the birds chirping outside or sense that the sun is starting to come up (though you should ideally have light-blocking shades!), and it can be tempting to just throw in the towel, get a cup of coffee, and turn on the early morning news. Try to resist doing this. Instead, consider any time between your set bedtime and set wake- time as the *middle of the night*. Ideally, you shouldn't be looking at a clock and know what time it is anyways, so really treat any time before the wake-up time as nighttime. If you wake up earlier than then from time to time, get up, take a shower, have some food or coffee, turn on lights, or watch TV, you're only sending a signal to your body that the sun has come up and the day has started. Your body's circadian rhythm will start to shift to the earlier time because you will have trained it to wake up early by engaging in awake and alerting activities.

Problem 7: I Just Can't Bring Myself to Get Out of My Cozy Bed at Night

To help motivate yourself, get some index cards (or bigger pieces of paper if needed) and write down phrases like "Short-term pain for long term gain and "Get out of bed and you'll kick your insomnia." Put them next to your bed or tape them to your door or even where you plan to go sit to follow stimulus control. This helps you override the irrational thinking that might get in the way of you following through with these guidelines in the middle of the night.

RETURNING TO EMILY

In my first treatment session with Emily, we discussed the same sleep hygiene basics mentioned in Chapter 8 of this book, as well as stimulus control. She was extremely resistant to getting out of bed, mostly for the fear of losing sleepiness if she got up. She had had insomnia for quite some time, so we discussed how this conditioning developed over the years and that she would have to commit to a good 2–4 weeks of consistent stimulus control to make a difference. Her insomnia did not start overnight, so there's no reason she should expect it to be cured overnight.

Once Emily realized that she would begin to fall asleep on the couch only to be completely awake when she got in bed, she could see how this conditioning theory applied to her: in her mind, her bed was only about rest and frustration. She committed to trying stimulus control, consistently, for 4 weeks. She was asked to wake up at 6:30 a.m. daily and to use an alarm 7 days a week. Emily brainstormed things to do at night if she was unable to sleep and had a plan set up for when she would use them. If she was unable to sleep in the early part of the night, she would sit on the couch reading a paper book about art history that she found interesting but not gripping. If she awoke in the middle of the night or early morning, she would get up, put on a robe and slippers, and sit on the couch in dim light reading her favorite celebrity and style magazines.

By week 3, Emily began to notice that she wasn't worrying as much in bed as she had in the past and was falling asleep faster because she was timing getting in bed with when she was actually sleepy. At times when she awoke in the middle of the night with an active, worried mind, the simple (though tough at first!) act of getting up and out of bed to read magazines helped quiet her brain and body. Eventually, by week 4, she found that she awoke less at night and rarely had trouble with falling asleep, resulting in less need to get out of bed, since she was now sleeping better.

Takeaway Message: Stimulus Control

- ✓ The bed is only for sleep and sex.
- ✓ If you can't sleep at any point between your bedtime and wake time, get up after a short while (*don't* look at the clock, just estimate around 20 minutes).
- ✓ Go to a different room, or at least a different area, and do something quiet, calm, and relaxing in dim light that passes the time.
- ✓ Find activities that work best for you that aren't too stimulating (such as reading, knitting, scrapbooking, or relaxation or mindfulness exercises).
- ✓ Return to bed only if you're sleepy.
- ✓ If you get back into bed and sleep doesn't come, repeat the exercise: get out of bed again, and return to bed again only if you're sleepy.
- ✓ Stick with it on a nightly basis—consistency is what works here!

FORM 9.1: Am I Sleepy? Fatigued? Both?

Check all that apply, on both sides of the form. If you think you have issues with daytime sleepiness (especially undesired or easily obtained dozing during the day), consider further evaluation by a sleep specialist.

Signs of Fatigue (common when only insomnia is present)	Signs of Sleepiness (common when there's another sleep or mood disorder, such as restless legs syndrome, sleep apnea, or depression)
☐ Dragging ☐ Sluggishness ☐ Mental fog/cloudiness ☐ Not able to nap even though desired (or it takes a long time to do so) ☐ No energy ☐ Tired but wired (brain is very much awake)	☐ Struggle to keep eyes open and stay awake ☐ Low energy, heaviness in limbs ☐ Lapses in alertness, unintentional dozing, head nodding ☐ Easily able to nap when desired ☐ Can't keep eyes open ☐ Struggle to stay awake in monotonous, quiet activities ☐ Eyes tearing

10.

Spend Less Time in Bed to Sleep More

Jody, a 68-year-old married woman, began having issues with her sleep once she retired 8 months ago. She managed to be a great sleeper for most of her life and noted that she struggled only when each of her three daughters (now all in their thirties) were babies. She managed to transition into menopause without much issue besides occasional hot flashes and is relatively healthy overall, with no major health concerns or significant anxiety or depression. She was self-employed as an attorney and made her own hours, but she got busier as the years went on and her children grew up. She made little time for sleep, often going to bed as late as midnight after a long day of work and waking up at 6 a.m. every morning to exercise. She occasionally slept later on the weekends in an attempt to catch up on lost sleep. Jody's husband was also an attorney and had retired a few years earlier. He had been encouraging his wife to retire along with him so that they could reduce life stress, travel, and spend more time with the children and grandchildren. Jody very much wanted to do this but struggled with the idea of leaving behind the busy practice she built for herself from the ground up and was unsure what she would do with herself on a day-to-day basis once she retired.

Although she was initially reluctant to do so, she eventually agreed to retire with the initial goal of relaxation and health improvement. Without any set routine from day to day, Jody went to bed whenever she felt like it and would get up whenever she would naturally awaken. After a few months, she increasingly found herself having trouble falling asleep or awakening in the middle of the night, tossing and turning in bed and ruminating about whether or not she had made the right decision to retire. She started to sleep in some mornings to try to catch up on sleep whenever she could. She exercised much less than before since she was tired and felt like she didn't have the energy. Over time, she found she was relying more and more on a glass of wine at night to relax and had considered asking her doctor for prescription sleep medication. Jody's baseline sleep diary is shown in Form 10.1 (remember, one week of baseline data is fine, though two weeks is really ideal).

SLEEP RESTRICTION THERAPY

Recall to the discussion of the two-process model of sleep in Chapter 2, especially the need to build up a sleep drive, or "sleep hunger" during the day to sleep well at night? We are going to put that theory to work here by using *sleep restriction* (Spielman, Saskin, & Thorpy, 1987), applying it to Jody's case as an example.

As a quick refresher, the concept of *sleep drive* is that the more you stay awake during the day, ideally the more you will sleep at night. This is exactly why we in the sleep field frown on napping for many people who have insomnia, especially naps after 2 p.m. and any naps longer than 20–30 minutes. Naps later in the day and/or longer in duration reduce the sleep drive at night, making it either difficult to fall asleep or challenging to stay asleep throughout the night. Think of sleep hunger like building up an appetite before dinner: if you have a snack too close to dinner, your appetite will be reduced or even spoiled, depending on how large and late the snack happened. The same is true with sleep.

You may also recall from Chapter 3 that common sense tends to take over—wrongfully so—when poor sleep takes hold and encourages us to go to bed earlier or sleep in later, with the thought that *today will be the day I'll get those glorious 8 hours of sleep.* We begin to engage in sleep extension: going to bed early or laying in bed later in the morning, hoping to catch up on lost sleep. The problem here is that, although it might work on occasion, it is typically an ineffective strategy overall to obtain good sleep on a consistent basis. What usually happens is you get *too much* sleep from those one or two nights, which then backfires, and you have a rougher time sleeping the next few nights. I like to think of it as a game of catch-up: a good night, then a few bad nights, then a good night or two with too much sleep, then a string of bad nights. It turns into a roller coaster and can make you dread each night as it gets closer, since you never know what you're going to get.

Sleep extension is one of the biggest common sense mistakes that we make, and understandably so. When you're in the throes of insomnia, your body will produce only a set average amount of sleep on a regular basis. This is precisely why tracking your sleep (even if not exact!) in a sleep diary for 2 weeks before beginning other treatment strategies is helpful: you will see just how much sleep, on average, your body will produce for the week. Sure, some nights may involve more sleep, and others less. That's why we average it across the week, to give you a good overall baseline.

Many people with insomnia have an ideal number of hours of sleep that they believe they need on a regular basis. It almost feels as if it is painted in gold and put up on a pedestal: the ideal trophy to obtain after a perfect night. However, that number typically does not jibe with the average number of hours of sleep their body is producing on a regular basis during a bout of insomnia. Every night, there's essentially a fight between the mind, saying, *I'm going to give you X number of hours in bed tonight, and you better sleep close to that many hours,* and the body, saying, *I don't care how much time you give me in bed, I'm only going to give you Y hours of sleep tonight!*

Sleep restriction works because we let go of what the mind desires and instead meet the body close to where it is, rather than fighting it at the outset. Once we accept where the body is in the present moment, we gradually train the body to give us more sleep. In the beginning, you spend a little *less* time in bed (TIB) to build up your sleep drive, and then you can obtain more consolidated, deeper sleep on a regular basis.

Many patients are skeptical when I explain it in session (and, in full disclosure, I was a skeptic at first myself), but it works for a lot of people. Sleep restriction is a very well-researched insomnia strategy and an overall treatment standard. I've seen it work for many, many women. Yes, this goes against common sense and can be tough to do at first, but it tends to get easier over time. Remember, consistency is so important, and keeping the same sleep schedule, night after night, regardless of whether or not you *think* tonight will be the night you can actually get those 8 hours, will be one of the best ways to achieve overall success.

An Initial Few Words of Caution

For some people (but not all!), the first few weeks of sleep restriction may create some mild sleep deprivation that might make you a bit more sleepy during the day than usual—a very unusual feeling for many patients with insomnia! This is a good thing for most people as it means you're building up an appetite for sleep, something that hadn't been there for a while. Be aware of your level of sleepiness (remember, not just fatigue—recall the difference from Chapter 9), and avoid driving, using heavy machinery, or engaging in any potentially dangerous activities until you are no longer excessively sleepy. Remember, it took time to develop insomnia, and it takes some time to reverse it, so be patient.

A note of caution: Although sleep restriction has been used effectively with patients who have bipolar disorder, parasomnias (such as sleep walking, sleep talking, night terrors, sleep sex disorder, confusional arousals), and seizure disorders, if you have one of these conditions you should consult with a behavioral sleep medicine specialist before you start regarding the extent to which you can restrict your sleep. For some people, sleep restriction may reduce the threshold for these events and may increase the risk of a manic episode, parasomnia episode, or seizure. As you will see, I never limit those with insomnia to less than 5 hours in bed at night. However, if you have any of the conditions just mentioned, your allowed time in bed (TIB) window will likely be larger—6.5 hours or even more, depending on the severity of your case. It does not mean you cannot do sleep restriction; it just means you need to be careful and possibly less restrictive with your allowed sleep/wake window.

Sleep restriction creates a consistent sleep/wake schedule based on your average total sleep need for the week, allowing you to prime your sleep drive to induce sleepiness and achieve continuous ("compressed") nighttime sleep. Once you know your sleep statistics from your baseline sleep diary, you can create an individualized plan for meeting your body where it is in the current state and then slowly train it to give you more sleep. (If you haven't done your baseline sleep diary, go back to Chapter 7 and follow the instructions there; then return to this chapter.)

Step 1: Use Your Baseline Sleep Statistics to Create an Initial Sleep Schedule

Take a look at your baseline sleep diary and the sleep stats at the bottom that you calculated at the end of the week. What was your average total sleep time (TST)? And your average sleep efficiency percentage (SE%)? For the first week of sleep restriction, we are concerned mostly with the TST value; SE% will be our primary guide for the weeks that follow.

To set your initial prescribed sleep/wake schedule, it is much easier to start with a consistent wake-up time on a regular basis than to start with bedtime. So start with your wake time, and then count back the number of TST hours to get your bedtime. For example, if you have 4 days per week when you need to be up at 6 a.m. and then the remaining days of the week you can wake up whenever you'd like, your goal wake-up time should ideally be 6 a.m. *every single morning, even on the weekends* (recall from Chapter 9 that a consistent wake time, 7 days a week, is crucial to obtaining a solid night's sleep on a regular basis). Of course, there may be days now and then when you might have to get up earlier for some reason, and that's OK. Do your best to keep a consistent wake time as many days as possible. Your body's circadian rhythm does not know which days are the "wake-early" days and which ones are not.

There is no ideal same wake time for everyone. Some people prefer to get up later, and some prefer earlier. Set your wake time based on your life's circumstances and personal preferences. If you have to get up for a class most days of the week at 7 a.m., then that should be your set wake time every day, for now. If you are retired and want to sleep until 8 a.m., then by all means, set that as your wake time every morning. Just remember to keep it realistic—if you are frequently up by 7 a.m. but would love to sleep late, it might not be easy to shift your sleep schedule to wake up hours later. The key here is to set a realistic wake time based on your life, one that you can keep consistently.

Now that you've chosen your same wake time (remember, for 7 days a week), look at your baseline diary's average TST for the past 2 weeks. Use that number to count backward from your wake time, and then add an extra 30-minute cushion, to create your allowed bedtime and TIB. For example, if your average TST for the past 2 weeks on your baseline sleep diary is 6 hours, and you want to wake up every morning at 7 a.m., count back the 6 hours from 7 a.m., which puts you at 1 a.m.; then, for good measure, add an extra 30 minutes, giving you a "prescribed" allowed TIB window of 12:30 a.m. to 7 a.m. This will be your TIB every night for the next week.

Note: Set the alarm for 7 a.m. *every* morning. Make friends with your alarm clock, even if you think you'll never need it—there might be that one morning when you sleep past your set wake time, and that would steal sleep from the next night.

Start a new sleep diary, and track your sleep on the new schedule for the next week. At the end of the week, you will reevaluate your sleep statistics and make a new sleep plan based on your new sleep statistics, using the same technique described above. Week by week your schedule will gradually change until you are getting the compressed sleep you need.

As a concrete example, let's have a look at Jody's baseline sleep diary (Form 10.1). When she calculated her sleep statistics for the week, her average TST was 6 hours and 20 minutes. After careful consideration, she decided she wanted to wake up at 7 a.m. daily so she could try to get in a morning walk with her husband while the weather was cooler outside. With her wake time set, she counted back 6 hours 20 minutes, which gave her a bedtime of 12:40 a.m. After adding the extra 30-minute cushion, her prescribed sleep window was 12:10 a.m. to 7 a.m. every night for the next week.

You might notice on Jody's baseline sleep diary that her TIB was typically between 8 and 10 hours each night, often at inconsistent bed and wake times. With her new prescribed sleep schedule of 12:10 a.m. to 7:00 a.m. every day, she had a structured time for her sleep, and her alarm clock would go off at 7 a.m. every morning. She then tracked her sleep on a new sleep diary sheet for her first week on the restricted sleep schedule (Form 10.2).

The other basic behavioral strategies apply even when you're implementing sleep restriction. Try to avoid any sleep outside of your set sleep/wake window—not even short naps. Don't get into bed until you're sleepy—not just tired but truly sleepy (yawning, heavy feeling in eyes or limbs). If you aren't sleepy at your allowed bedtime, continue to stay awake doing your quiet, calm, and relaxing wind-down activity in dim light (see Chapter 8 for a review) until you get sleepy. Then get in bed. If you are in bed and unable to sleep at any point during your allowed sleep/wake window, continue to follow the rules of stimulus control (see Chapter 9 for a refresher): get up, do something quiet, calm, and relaxing in dim light until you're sleepy again, and then get back into bed. Remember, the bed is only for sleep and sex. And make sure to get up and out of bed at your prescribed wake time—do not stay in bed after that time, no matter how many hours you slept the night before.

Step 2: Modify Your Sleep/Wake Schedule Based on Your Stats

Now that you've been keeping a prescribed, consistent sleep/wake schedule, you may already find some improvement in your sleep. Or you might notice that there hasn't been any change and you're tired. Some people feel better right away, and others tend to feel worse for a few initial weeks before they improve. Many people begin behavioral insomnia treatments many months or even years after first developing sleep problems, and it takes time to undo that pattern, so patience is extremely important here. Sleep restriction can sometimes take 2–3 weeks of consistent implementation to see improvements. Give it a few weeks, and be as patient as possible.

Look at your sleep diary for the past week with the prescribed TIB. Were you able to keep it? What were your struggles? Calculate your average SE% for this first sleep-restricted week—from here on, SE% will be your guide to modify the TIB (as opposed to TST, which we used the first week).

If your SE% average for the past week was 90 percent or more, you're doing *really* well. This suggests that 90 percent of most nights this week you were in bed and sleeping during the allowed sleep schedule. If your SE% is 90 percent or more, go to bed 15 minutes earlier the next week. Remember, in Step 1 we met your body where it was with TST; now we're letting SE% be our guide to training your body to give you more sleep. Gradual changes tend to work best for most people, so your bedtime will be earlier by not more than 15 minutes every week.

If the SE% average is between 85 and 90 percent, your body is telling you that there's some improvement but not enough to open up the sleep window just yet. Stay at the current sleep/wake schedule one more week and let your body adjust. Then, reassess the next week to see if you can open up the sleep window. Don't change a thing for the next week.

If the SE% is 85 percent or less on average for the past week, go to bed 15 minutes later for the next week. The wake time stays the exact same as usual, but the bedtime gets slightly more restricted. **Note:** Don't limit yourself to less than 5 hours TIB, even if your average TST is less than that; if you've had a 5 hour prescribed sleep window for the past week and your SE% average for the week was less than 85 percent, stay at the 5 hour window—don't limit it any further.

After you've made the sleep window prescription for the upcoming week, based on your SE% average for the past week's restriction, track your sleep yet again on a new page in your sleep diary, and the next week make the same types of adjustments. Table 10.1 summarizes the guidelines for using average SE% to adjust your sleep window each week.

Note: When you're starting to sleep a bit better, you are likely going to become anxious to increase your allowed sleep window by more than 15 minutes each week. This is when you need to be patient. In my clinical experience over the years, I've found that increasing the allowed TIB window by small, 15-minute increments each week slowly trains the body in giving you more sleep. Any faster and you risk things going off course.

TABLE 10.1: Guidelines for Next Week's Prescribed Time in Bed (Once You've Set Your Initial Prescribed TIB in Step 1)

SE% Average for the Past Week	TIB Adjustment for the Next Week
≥90%	Go to bed 15 minutes earlier for the next week; wake time stays the same every morning.
86–89%	Stay on the same sleep/wake schedule for the next week.
≤85%	Go to bed 15 minutes later for the next week; wake time stays the same every morning.

Now let's apply Step 2 to Jody. Based on her sleep diary from the first week of sleep restriction (Form 10.2), she was very good at keeping her 12:10 a.m. to 7 a.m. sleep/wake schedule. She calculated her sleep stats for the week, and her SE% weekly average was 92 percent; based on the guidelines in Table 10.1, this allows her to go to bed 15 minutes earlier for the next week. So, her new bedtime is set for 11:55 p.m., and the wake time remains the same, at 7 a.m. She will then track her sleep again on another sleep diary page for the next week on this new sleep schedule, and then reevaluate again in one week's time by calculating her sleep stats for that next week.

You might be comparing Jody's baseline sleep diary and her follow-up diary, asking yourself why she's getting a little less sleep on the follow-up week (6 hours, 15 minutes) than the baseline week (6 hours, 20 minutes) and questioning why this is even beneficial. Remember, we might create a small amount of sleep deprivation here to compress sleep at night. Her baseline SE% was 75 percent, suggesting that her sleep was quite broken throughout the night and not very consolidated. Think of it like she was "snacking" on sleep throughout the night instead of having a satisfying meal. Once we created a consistent and somewhat restricted schedule for her, the SE% increased to 92 percent, signaling to us right away that we are on the right track to consolidating and deepening her sleep at night. Now, we move onto Step 3.

Step 3: Continue to Adjust the TIB Window Until You're Satisfied

At the end of each week, take a look at your sleep diary and calculate your sleep stats. Using the guidelines from Step 2, adjust your prescribed sleep window based on your SE% for the previous week, repeating this week after week. Again, the wake time ideally stays the same every week during active sleep restriction, and you modify the bedtime week after week. You might have some weeks when your SE% goes down and your TIB is shortened by 15 minutes, some weeks when it stays the same, and others when your SE% goes up and you add 15 minutes to the sleep window; overall, you should slowly increase your TST. Remember, right now it is more about the quality of your sleep, compressing your sleep at night, than about your TIB or TST.

The sticking point for most patients is when to end sleep restriction: at what sleep window will you finally stop? Some patients want to know ahead of time exactly how much sleep they'll end up getting on a nightly basis once sleep restriction is done. This is a hard question to answer—it really does vary from person to person. Instead, follow your body's cues at the end of each week and keep opening up your sleep window if you have an SE% average of 90 percent or above. Keep opening the window week after week until you find your SE% average drops—if you open the bedtime window by another 15 minutes and find that your SE% average drops for the next week, it is possible that you have gone too far. If your SE% average improves when you tighten up the schedule a bit and you generally feel well rested and refreshed for most of the day, you've likely settled on the sleep/wake schedule that you should stay with for the time being.

It is important to remember here that your body's sleep need may differ from what you *think* you need. Although you may have heard that 8 hours is ideal, your body might have a different number in mind. That is why we follow the stats you record in your sleep diary: reevaluate what you need to do based on the SE% average for that week, and then modify the bedtime window as needed (by 15 minutes later or earlier, or even just stay the same, based on the SE% guidelines). Go with how you feel more than by a number painted in gold, sitting on a pedestal high in the air. Make changes to your TIB on a weekly basis, and if you find you start stalling out after a few weeks, you may have just opened up your bedtime too much.

TROUBLESHOOTING AND MODIFICATIONS
FOR SLEEP RESTRICTION

As is the case with stimulus control (for a review, see Chapter 9), the theory and guidelines for sleep restriction are straightforward. The real work comes in thinking ahead and troubleshooting any problems that may arise. I commonly see people who are given sleep restriction rules by various doctors, but they're not given ways to help troubleshoot the inevitable issues that likely get in the way of properly following the treatment. Here are some of the most common problems women have reported when doing sleep restriction.

Problem 1: It Just Isn't Working!

Often, women will come to my office after a few weeks saying that they tried sleep restriction, sleep hygiene, and stimulus control and that it just isn't working. After some discussion, we typically find areas where they can follow the treatment rules better. Although sleep restriction and stimulus control each work on their own for many people, I have found in my work with patients that they work better, and faster, when combined.

If you're struggling with following everything at once, first make sure you're doing at least one of the behavioral modules as written. Start with sleep tracking. Are you tracking your sleep nightly and practicing proper sleep hygiene overall? If so, then make sure you're doing stimulus control regularly. Once stimulus control is on solid ground, then work on tightening up your ability to follow sleep restriction. If you're following—as written!—stimulus control and sleep restriction for a month and you're not getting any better at all, continue on to the cognitive techniques in Part 3 of this book, as they may be of additional help. You may want to consider sticking with behavioral and cognitive strategies combined for a few more weeks, as data suggests that adding cognitive and mindfulness techniques can bolster overall effects.

However, if you are fully following the behavioral recommendations and are noticing no gains whatsoever after a month, or you find your symptoms are worsening after a few weeks' time, you might want to think about switching strategies: just focusing on cognitive techniques or mindfulness, or limiting your behavioral approach to just sleep hygiene and stimulus control while trying cognitive/mindfulness techniques described in Part 3. Finally, if you feel that you're struggling with these instructions or that you are unsure if it is right for you, consider seeking the help from a clinician who is well versed in CBT-I.

Problem 2: I Simply Can't Stay Awake Until My Prescribed Bedtime

This is an extremely common (and surprising!) problem since many women with insomnia rarely experience significant sleepiness (until sleep restriction is initiated). An irony to consider here is that if you're reading this book due to issues with falling asleep at the beginning of the night, and now you're wondering how you'll stay awake until the new prescribed bedtime, well, congrats! Your sleep is improving!!! You were initially reading this book because of problems with falling asleep when you got in bed at bedtime. Now, with your new prescribed later bedtime and set wake time, you're actually *struggling* to stay awake until the time you're supposed to go to bed! The question has switched from *how can I fall asleep?* to *how can I stay awake?*

However, if you mostly have issues with waking up in the middle of the night or getting up too early in the morning, and are not having issues at bedtime, you can't congratulate yourself just yet, since staying awake is definitely necessary to strengthen your sleep drive, eventually allowing you to sleep longer and more consolidated throughout the night.

Remember, all naps, even small dozes for a few seconds (aka microsleep episodes) here and there in the evening, can reduce your sleep drive. The first thing to consider is how you are spending your evening before your set bedtime that might lead to your dozing episodes or excessive sleepiness. Are you in a dimly lit room? Are you sitting on a couch or in a chair with your feet up, head comfortably resting on a pillow and watching TV or reading? Worse yet, are you lying down on your couch? I have yet to work with someone who purposefully purchases an uncomfortable couch to unwind on at night before bed.

Keep your room brightly lit until 1 hour before your bedtime, and figure out if you have any "sleepy" triggers. Is it the cozy shawl over your shoulders? If so, don't use it. Is it the recliner in the den? If so, sit in a different chair. Some patients have had success sitting in a hard-backed chair such as a dining room chair since it does not allow them to recline.

Also, consider the length of time that you're sitting in this position. For example, if your new prescribed bedtime is 2:00 a.m. and you're used to starting your wind-down routine at 7:30 p.m. every night with the rest of your family, you're winding down for bed and being sedentary far too early for your new delayed sleep restriction bedtime. There's no need to spend over 6 hours winding down before bedtime.

Instead, I encourage you to try to reframe the later bedtime as a way to get things done that you usually do not have time to do, such as doing things for yourself that you never make time for in your busy life. Do you have young kids at home and relish those few quiet hours after they go to bed? Or do you work late most nights and never have time to decompress after making lunch for the next day, doing dishes, and cleaning up the house? Make use of this extra time at night because, if your insomnia starts to resolve and you begin to add time to your allowed sleep window every week, you might not have these extra few hours at night for long!

Keep your environment bright and active up until 1 hour before bed. Then you can start to fully wind down and dim the lights and electronics. You can engage in extra work, pay bills, do housework, whatever you'd like in these extra hours, but I do encourage you to use this time for more relaxing activities or tasks that you simply never have time accomplish. Stress management is extremely important in our fast-paced lives as women with multiple roles; we rarely carve out enough time for our own needs. The activities you can choose to do are vast and varied. You can clean out kitchen cupboards for cans to donate to the local food pantry. Or organize and clean out closets and dressers. Or use the time to learn new hobbies and skills: new languages, knitting, painting, jigsaw puzzles, sudoku, crossword puzzles, scrapbooking, using computer photo editing software or adult coloring books, and playing the keyboard.

You can even use this time to catch up on the latest TV shows, movies, or books that you haven't been able to get around to with life pulling you in so many ways. It is totally fine to engage in these relaxing behaviors, but make sure that you do not doze (even for a few minutes!) during these activities. If you are prone to fall asleep while watching TV but really want to do so, maybe dust a bit while watching TV, or fold some laundry, do a puzzle, or knit. Sit in a well-lit place where you are less likely to doze. One hour before bed, though, dim all lights, block the screen use, and wind down. If you are still struggling to stay awake even with the one-hour wind down, cut the wind-down time to 20–30 minutes instead. It is important to wind down, but going to bed later to prime the sleep drive by avoiding dozing is very important here, and I would rather you sacrifice a small amount of wind-down time (though not all!) to help you stay awake to the desired sleep restriction prescribed bedtime.

If you choose to use some of the time to do chores around the house but are worried that you are too tired to do anything at night, consider flipping some of the chores you do earlier in the day to later at night. For example, a lot of people may do dishes, dust, do laundry, or vacuum in the morning or early afternoon, at times when they typically have more energy to do these activities. If you think more about it, though, it is highly likely that even in the late evening you can still sit on the couch and fold some laundry or sit in front of a drawer and pull out sweaters to be stored away for winter.

Problem 3: I Wake Up Earlier Than My Alarm Clock Is Set for Every Morning

Waking up too early is a common concern for many women suffering from insomnia. If that happens, consider it just as if it is still the middle of the night. Try as best you can to not look at the clock—that's why you have an alarm clock set, to let you know that the morning time has come and you can start your day. Follow the basic stimulus control rules if you are unable to fall back asleep. Even if you think it is close to an hour of your waking up (you might hear some birds chirping outside or hear your heater turn on), still consider it the middle of the night until the alarm clock has gone off. Get up, if you can't fall back asleep, and do something quiet, calm, and relaxing in dim light outside the bed area. Return to bed if you get sleepy again, but even if you only get a minute of sleep before the alarm goes off, get up when you hear the alarm clock.

Try not to start your day before the time you've set your alarm to go off. Often, women who wake up earlier than they'd like will get up, take a shower, make coffee, eat breakfast, watch TV, do household chores, and have all the lights on before they need to be awake. Doing "awake" activities earlier than you desire to be awake only trains your body to start awakening earlier to do these things.

Problem 4: My Physical Condition Just Won't Let Me Stay Up That Late

Often older adults and patients who have issues with chronic pain or other significant medical issues that impact their ability to sleep throughout the night struggle with the 90 percent cutoff rule and significantly later bed times. A common modification for sleep restriction in these cases is to reduce the SE% cutoff points for sleep restriction, as shown in Table 10.2; for example, instead of using an SE% average of 90 percent as the cutoff to be able to increase your bedtime by 15 minutes for the next week, use 85 percent instead.

TABLE 10.2: **Guidelines for Next Week's Prescribed Time in Bed: Modifications for Older Adults and Those With Chronic Pain Issues (Once You've Set Your Initial Prescribed TIB in Step 1)**

SE% Average for the Past Week	TIB Adjustment for the Next Week
≥85%	Go to bed 15 minutes earlier for the next week; wake time stays the same every morning.
81–84%	Stay on the same sleep/wake schedule for the next week.
≤80%	Go to bed 15 minutes later for the next week; wake time stays the same every morning.

Another consideration for some people, especially older adults who struggle with staying awake significantly later to the prescribed bedtime, is to practice sleep compression instead of sleep restriction. *Sleep compression* is a more gradual, looser form of sleep restriction where, instead of immediately restricting yourself to a rigid TIB based on your average TST for the week, you set a rigid wake time daily and try to go to bed 30–60 minutes later each week. Think of it like ripping off a bandage: you can do it quickly and get it over with (sleep restriction) or slowly but have some more pain along the way (sleep compression)—either way, you end up with the same result.

There's no hard-and-fast rule with sleep compression besides setting a fixed wake time and trying to go to bed later each week. How late you decide to go to bed depends on what you can manage (often patients will do 30–60 minutes later bedtimes each week), but it is ideal to set a slightly compressed schedule and keep it for one week. Fill out your sleep diary throughout the week, and then reevaluate and compress a bit more the next week (keeping the wake time the same each week)—keep compressing each week by 30–60 minutes, keeping the same sleep schedule nightly for the week, and eventually you will restrict yourself enough that sleep will start consolidating at night. Then you can begin opening up the bedtime window by 15 minutes every week or so, following Steps 2 and 3 of sleep restriction.

Problem 5: What If I'm Still Taking Sleep Aids?

Ideally, you should stop taking sleep medications before doing sleep restriction, but many people find it extremely difficult to stop all sleep medications without other tools to help them sleep better and prefer to combine both treatments. For many people, it can be hard to follow both stimulus control and sleep restriction when on sedating medications.

It is extremely important that you talk with your doctor before beginning sleep restriction, as it can be a balancing act between properly timing your medication and completing sleep restriction. A number of newer sleep medications require that you take them at least 8 hours before you start your day or you risk being drowsy during morning activities. Talk with your doctor about the ideal time to take your medication since with sleep restriction it is likely you will be in bed for less than 8 hours. Be sure not to engage in any activities that could become dangerous if you are drowsy (driving, operating heavy machinery, caring for little children).

If you plan to make any changes to your sleep medications, such as tapering your dose, while doing sleep restriction at the same time, it is best to talk with your doctor as well, since changing your prescribed sleep window *and* reducing your sleep medications at the same time can be complicated. That's not to say it can't be done—it is just best to get a taper guideline from your doctor first and make sure not to change your sleep schedule at the same time you change your medication dose. Sleep medications also affect stimulus control: some patients find that the medication wears off so fast that they have no issue with getting out of bed to go read in another room, whereas others feel quite loopy and struggle with just sitting up in bed to make some demarcation between wake activities and sleep.

I personally prefer patients keep their sleep medication dose the same while they optimize their sleep and remain that way for at least 1–2 weeks. Then they taper with their doctor's approval to a lower dose. This usually disrupts sleep again, and sleep restriction is reinitiated, meeting the body where it is on the lower medication dose. Once sleep is optimized again on this lower dose, wait a few more weeks and then drop the dose again, but only with the guidance of your doctor.

Problem 6: What If My Bed Partner Wants Me to Come to Bed When She or He Goes to Bed?

Some partners want to go to bed together so they can spend quality time together. But quality time can be spent anywhere and does not need to be in bed. If your loved one is truly invested in your getting better, involve him or her in your strategies and explain the reasons behind your needing to do what is outlined in this book. Routines can be extremely comforting for many couples, but if they stop working for the person with insomnia and only worsen the dread about being in the bed, then why do you continue them? Is it out of concern for not hurting your loved one's feelings? Fear of how he or she will respond? Far too frequently, I see women in my practice defer to their husband's sleep schedule and bedroom preferences as "he needs to go to bed early" or "wake up late" and they're too "worried about disturbing his sleep." Why is your sleep any less important than his? Try to come up with a compromise that works for you both and does not bring up resentment.

Research has found that upward of 74 percent of partners encouraged early bed or later wake times for their insomnia-suffering loved ones (Mellor et al., 2017). As we've discussed, common sense and insomnia don't mix: "You must be so tired, come to bed early," "You didn't sleep well last night, sleep later this morning," or "Come take a nap" are very routine thoughts for both those with insomnia and their friends and family. But the reality, as I hope you understand by now, is that this can perpetuate the problem.

I've had some patients with bed partners that need to sleep in a much warmer room, or can only sleep with the lights on, and there's little area to find compromise for a good sleep environment. In these rare circumstances, these patients have made the choice to sleep in separate beds or separate rooms, and many found it quite refreshing. In some instances, it can get rid of resentment and arguing over the sleep environment and allow for better sleep for both partners and a closer relationship. Let's be honest, this option is not for everyone, and the pros/cons of this option need to be weighed quite carefully and considerately as a couple. If you choose to go this route, modify the stimulus control instructions somewhat. Pick one bed to have some closeness/cuddle time in for a short while (20 minutes or so) before bed, have sex if you desire, but when it is time for sleep, go to your own beds.

If your bed partner is completely unwilling to change his or her mindset and refuses to turn off the TV at night, must sleep with the lights on, or other things that might disturb to your sleep, then a more serious conversation needs to be had about respect for each other's health and well-being.

Problem 7: What If I Sleep Through My Alarm?

Some patients with insomnia report that they get their best sleep in the early morning hours, close to the time the alarm clock goes off. This is precisely why it is important to become good friends with your alarm clock and not sleep in. If you do sleep in, you won't be setting a good sleep/wake schedule and risk bigger problems for the next few nights.

Sometimes, though, patients will be in such a deep sleep in the early morning hours that they simply don't hear their alarm clock. If this is a problem, first consider what kind of alarm clock you have. Is it a faint radio alarm? If so, make it louder or somewhat more annoying. Also consider using two or more alarms, having one go off and another about 5 minutes later. A silent vibrating pillow alarm, a watch alarm, or even ear-bud alarms are very handy for some patients, especially those who worry about waking up a bed partner with a different sleep schedule.

Do you often forget to set your alarm? If so, find one that has a repeating alarm. Maybe you tablet computer and smartphone has this option, but be careful about keeping tech in your room, as it can be quite tempting to roll over and look at it throughout the night. If typical alarms aren't working, consider downloading an app for your phone or tablet that won't turn off until you solve a word or math puzzle—these can be extremely effective for many who struggle with getting up to their alarm.

If you are keeping to the sleep schedule that you have set and are still unable to awaken to an alarm in the morning on a regular basis, and possibly suffering from excessive daytime sleepiness, consider talking with a sleep specialist to rule out any other issues that might be affecting your sleep quality or circadian timing.

Problem 8: I Don't Want to Keep This Sleep Schedule Forever!

Try not to think of "forever" while doing this, and instead see it as a way to retrain your body clock. Often, women surprise themselves and find that they get used to the new sleep schedule over time and actually enjoy the quiet time after others in the house have gone to bed or before others wake up and start their day. Once you've improved your sleep and are on a consistent bedtime and wake-time schedule that feels good to you, there's a little bit of wiggle room with the weekends, but I do recommend not sleeping in more than an extra hour those days. If you go to bed late for some reason, try not to sleep too late the next morning and instead get up around the same time as usual, but take a short, 20-

minute nap later in the morning/early afternoon (before 2 p.m.) to help refresh yourself. Sleeping too late or going to bed too early is a slippery slope and can easily become a pattern where you set yourself up for a mismatch between the amount of time spent in bed and total time asleep. It is best to keep things as regular as possible, and if you have a night or two when you get off track, just make note of it, don't make a big deal out of it, and instead get back to the sleep schedule you were on before things got confused.

Takeaway Message: Sleep Restriction

- ✓ Sleep restriction can be challenging to implement consistently, but when used properly, it is one of the most beneficial strategies for insomnia currently available.
- ✓ Sleep restriction can easily be combined with many other behavioral and cognitive strategies for insomnia, but caution must be taken if you already use nighttime sedating medications (speak with your doctor for the best overall timing for taking these medications).
- ✓ Before starting sleep restriction, track your baseline sleep in a sleep diary for 1–2 weeks to see how much sleep you're getting, averaged across that time period.
- ✓ Use the guidelines in this chapter to determine your initial "sleep window" based on your sleep diary data; then week after week if your sleep diary shows you're improving, move your bedtime earlier by 15 minutes.
- ✓ Don't focus on a particular number of hours of sleep each night as your "goal" for sleep restriction—that can worsen your insomnia. Instead, stop sleep restriction once you've reached a sleep window where you feel happy with your sleep most nights each week (allowing for one or two nights weekly when it may not be ideal).

FORM 10.1: Jody's Baseline Sleep Diary

Fill Out Just Before Going to Bed at Night							
A. Day and date	Monday 2/4	Tuesday 2/5	Wednesday 2/6	Thursday 2/7	Friday 2/8	Saturday 2/9	Sunday 2/10
B. Naps	4–4:15 p.m.	—	2–2:45 p.m.	3–3:55 p.m.	—	10–11 a.m.	—
C. Exercise	—	—	1–1:50 p.m. walk	—	1–1:50 p.m. walk	—	—
D. Caffeine	Coffee: 8 oz 10 a.m.	—	Coffee: 8 oz 8 a.m.	Coffee: 8 oz 9 a.m.	—	Coffee: 8 oz 10 a.m.	Coffee: 8 oz 10 a.m.
E. Sleep medications or alcohol	1 glass wine 9 p.m.	1 glass wine 9 p.m.	2 glasses wine 8 p.m.	—	—	1 glass wine 8 p.m.	2 glasses wine 8 p.m.
F. Time you went to bed and turned out the lights	10 p.m.	11 p.m.	11 p.m.	10:30 p.m.	11 p.m.	11 p.m.	11 p.m.
Fill Out the Next Morning in Reference to the Night Before							
G. Time to fall asleep for first time	150 min	120 min	10 min	10 min	60 min	5 min	120 min
H. Number of awakenings in middle of night	2	3	4	1	1	1	2
I. Total time awake after falling asleep	120 min	90 min	90 min	20 min	20 min	10 min	20 min
J. Time you finally woke up	7:30 a.m.	7 a.m.	6:45 a.m.	8 a.m.	7 a.m.	7 a.m.	6:45 a.m.
K. Time you finally got out of bed	8:00 a.m.	7 a.m.	7 a.m.	8 a.m.	7 a.m.	7 a.m.	7 a.m.

Your Sleep Stats: Sleep Efficiency Calculation							
Total time in bed (TIB)	600 min	480 min	480 min	570 min	480 min	480 min	480 min
Total sleep time (TST)	300 min	270 min	365 min	540 min	400 min	465 min	325 min
Sleep efficiency (SE%): TST/TIB × 100	50%	56%	76%	95%	83%	97%	68%

AVERAGE TST $\quad$ = 300 + 270 + 365 + 540 + 400 + 465 + 325
$\qquad\qquad\quad$ = 2665/7
$\qquad\qquad\quad$ = 381 minutes (6 hours, 20 minutes)

AVERAGE SE% $\quad$ = 50% + 56% + 76% + 95% + 83% + 97% + 68%
$\qquad\qquad\quad$ = 75%

FORM 10.2: Jody's Sleep Diary—Week 1 of Sleep Restriction

Fill Out Just Before Going to Bed at Night							
A. Day and date	Monday 2/4	Tuesday 2/5	Wednesday 2/6	Thursday 2/7	Friday 2/8	Saturday 2/9	Sunday 2/10
B. Naps	4–4:15 p.m.	—	2–2:45 p.m.	3–3:55 p.m.	—	10–11 a.m.	—
C. Exercise	—	—	1–1:50 p.m. walk	—	1–1:50 p.m. walk	—	—
D. Caffeine	Coffee 8 oz 10 a.m.	—	Coffee: 8 oz 8 a.m.,	Coffee: 8 oz 9 a.m.	—	Coffee: 8 oz 10 a.m.	Coffee: 8 oz 10 a.m.
E. Sleep Medications or Alcohol	1 glass wine 9 p.m.	1 glass wine 9 p.m.	2 glasses wine 8 p.m.	—	—	1 glass wine 8 p.m.	2 glasses wine 8 p.m.
F. Time you went to bed and turned out the lights	12:10 a.m.	12:10 a.m.	12:10 a.m.	12:10 a.m.	12:10 a.m.	12:10 a.m.	12:10 a.m.

Fill Out the Next Morning in Reference to the Night Before							
G. Time to fall asleep for first time	60 min	30 min	2 min	10 min	20 min	5 min	20 min
H. Number of awakenings in middle of night	2	1	1	1	1	1	2
I. Total time awake after falling asleep	20 min	5 min	5 min	20 min	5 min	10 min	30 min
J. Time you finally woke up	7:00 a.m.	7:00 a.m.	7:00 a.m.	7:00 a.m.	7:00 a.m.	7:00 a.m.	7:00 a.m
K. Time you finally got out of bed	7:00 a.m.	7:00 a.m.	7:00 a.m.	7:00 a.m.	7:00 a.m.	7:00 a.m.	7:00 a.m
Your Sleep Stats: Sleep Efficiency Calculation							
Total time in bed (TIB)	410 min	410 min	410 min	410 min	410 min	410 min	410 min
Total sleep time (TST)	330 min	375 min	403 min	380 min	385 min	395 min	360 min
Sleep efficiency (SE%): TST/TIB × 100	81%	91%	98%	93%	94%	96%	88%

AVERAGE TST = 330 + 375 + 403 + 380 + 385 + 395 + 360
                      = 2628/7
                      = 375 minutes (6 hours, 15 minutes)

AVERAGE SE % = 81% + 91% + 98% + 93% + 94% + 96% + 88%
                      = 641%/7
                      = 92%

PART 3

Change Your Thoughts

11.

Change Your Thoughts for Better Sleep

Whether we realize it or not, we have countless thoughts per hour. Women's brains are often going and going, and sometimes they're going so fast and juggling so much that we don't even realize all the things we are thinking about in a given moment. However, if I stopped you in your tracks and asked you, "What were you thinking about this very second?," you can probably turn your attention to these thoughts (though it may take some practice), almost as if you're putting a spotlight on them. Often these thoughts are completely benign (such as "the walls in this room are yellow"). Sometimes, though, they're positive (such as "I love when my kids laugh and play") and other times quite negative (such as "I won't have any energy to play with my kids today because I didn't sleep last night").

Cognitive therapy, developed by Dr. Aaron Beck in the 1960s, is based on the belief that many times our thoughts are just that—thoughts. They're automatic and, surprisingly to some, not always rooted completely in reality. Even though they're *our* thoughts, they're filtered through the colored glasses through which we see the world. Sometimes—ideally many times—these thoughts are completely accurate, but there are times when they are not. Just as when positive thoughts typically lighten your mood, negative thoughts can bring your mood down, making you more anxious and sad—emotions that can typically interfere with a good night's sleep.

The cognitive model Beck developed, in essence, starts when we are presented with a situation. The situation leads to an automatic thought, and that thought (how we *perceive* the world) generates an emotion and then a behavior:

Cognitive model = Situation → Automatic thought → Emotion → Behavior

Table 11.1 gives some examples of the cognitive model in action. In these examples, the automatic thoughts generated by the various situations lead to significant negative emotions and detrimental behaviors. Often these behaviors worsen our mood, leading us to a downward spiral. Once you get better at recognizing your automatic thoughts, especially the ones that bring down your mood to make you sad or anxious, you can then work on evaluating them to see how accurate they are, thereby modifying your emotional and behavioral response.

Cognitive therapy is an extremely useful tool in many areas of psychology (such as depression and many types of anxiety disorders), and it has been applied to insomnia treatment, as well, since many patients with insomnia tend to have negative thoughts about their sleep at night and negative predictions about how the day will go after a poor night of sleep. Many women get caught in the cycle of worrying about whether they'll sleep that night and then become concerned about the daytime effects after a poor night's sleep. This in turn leads to more worry about whether they'll sleep, often making them try to force sleep to happen: *I must sleep tonight; otherwise, X, Y, and Z will happen tomorrow.* Forcing sleep to happen simply doesn't work—you can't will yourself to go to sleep; you can only set the stage for your brain and body to go to sleep. Cognitive therapy helps quiet the brain's worries and frustrations about sleep, thereby helping sleep to happen.

TABLE 11.1: **The Cognitive Model in Action**

Situation	Automatic Thought	Emotion	Behavior
Long-time friend calls to cancel on lunch date.	*She doesn't like me anymore. I must have done something to make her not like me.*	Sad, upset	Avoid calling friend for lunch dates in the future.
Make a mistake on a work report.	*I'm not good at my job and will get fired.*	Anxious, upset	Focus on the errors made, have even more difficulty focusing at work, and make more errors due to anxiety.
Watch TV in living room with husband at 9 p.m.	*I must sleep tonight. I have too much to do tomorrow and won't get anything done if I don't sleep.*	Anxious	Get in bed earlier to try to force sleep to happen, which leads to more tension and less sleep.
Awake at 4 a.m. staring at cell phone in bed.	*This is going to go on forever. I will never sleep, and tomorrow its going to be too hard to take care of my kids.*	Anxious, angry, hopeless	Get out of bed and start doing chores and paying bills on the computer to make use of the time awake.
Wake up in the morning after a night of tossing and turning.	*I won't be able to function today at work.*	Anxious, upset	Call out sick to work, continue lying in bed tossing and turning for a few more hours.

ADDRESSING NEGATIVE AUTOMATIC THOUGHTS

Now that you understand the cognitive model, let's work on applying cognitive therapy to any negative automatic thoughts you might have about your sleep or daytime functioning. There are three basic steps, each of which is discussed in detail below:

1. Use a Thought Challenge Form (Form 11.1) to identify your negative thoughts related to sleep or next day's performance/events.
2. Go through the Challenge Questions (Form 11.2) to evaluate your thoughts.
3. Create a Challenge Statement summary based on your questioning and write it on the Thought Challenge Form.

Step I: Identify Your Negative Thoughts on the Thought Challenge Form

We are often in tune with our emotions more than our thoughts. We often notice when we're feeling anxious, stressed, worried, sad, and upset but sometimes we aren't so aware of the thoughts that caused these emotions to arise. However, training yourself to turn your attention to your thoughts is not too difficult—it just takes some practice. When you notice your emotions take a turn for the worse, stop yourself in the moment and ask, *What was I just thinking when I experienced this emotion?*

The Thought Challenge Form (Form 11.1) can help you train yourself to become aware of thoughts that lead to negative emotions. When you initially notice a change in emotion toward the negative, immediately take out a blank Thought Challenge Form. Quickly jot down the date and situation. Next, jot down the mood that you're experiencing in that moment. Are you feeling sad? Anxious? Depressed? Irritable? Is it a combination of many emotions?

Now write down your negative thoughts and predictions, specifically ones related to sleep, lack of sleep, or what you think might happen because of a lack of sleep, as these are typically the thoughts that create the spiral related to worrying about sleep and then trying to force sleep to happen. It is important to note here that we sometimes have the tendency to temper our thoughts a bit when we write them down.

You might begin to find that you have similar thoughts in the same situations or at the same time of day (or both!). For example, I often hear women say that they dread the night as it gets closer, and once they put their kids down for bed they notice that negative thoughts about sleep begin to pop into mind.

All too frequently, I have women come in with Thought Challenge Forms that have questions written down instead of thoughts. For example, after a night of poor sleep, someone might write, "Will I be able to do my job tomorrow? Will I have any energy? Will I get through the day?" If the answers to these questions were in fact, "Yes, I will have energy. Yes, I will do fine at work. Yes I will get through the day," then the mood associated with the thoughts is likely not going to be negative. It is more plausible that these questions are statements when they go through your head, more along the lines of "I won't have any energy today" or "I'll struggle to get through work today." When you hear it this way, it becomes clearer that a negative emotion is associated with this thought (such as sadness, anger, or anxiety). So anytime you want to write down a question, see if you can flip it into a statement, since that's likely to have a more powerful emotion attached to it, a reason to bring out the Thought Challenge Form.

For more detailed example of how to fill out the first four columns, let's examine Judy's Thought Challenge Form (see Form 11.3). Judy is a 38-year-old stay-at-home mom to three kids, ages 5, 7, and 9. Although her kids are usually in school, they've been home on school break for the past 2 weeks and she's finding that her insomnia has made her more tired during the day, leading to increased anxiety at night and worsened sleep. She typically dreads the night as it gets closer, thinking, *Here I go again, another night of tossing and turning. If I don't sleep tonight, I won't be able to function tomorrow with my kids.* As nighttime grows closer, Judy's thoughts about not sleeping at night usually intensify, causing her to become even more anxious. This then leads to her lying in bed, tossing and turning, tense and with a busy mind, making sleep extremely difficult to obtain. In a way, her thought of *I won't sleep tonight* becomes a self-fulfilling prophecy; her anxiety about sleeping impacts her ability to relax and let sleep come on its own. Take a look at Form 11.3 to see how Judy completed Step 1 on her Thought Challenge Form.

Step 2: Go Through the Challenge Questions to Evaluate Your Thoughts

Now that you have filled out some thoughts on your Thought Challenge Form, the next step is to truly evaluate your thoughts and see whether or not they are totally accurate. I can't stress this enough: our thoughts are just that—thoughts. They're our perceptions of the world around us, almost as if we have on tinted glasses when viewing the world. Sometimes those glasses may be rose colored, other times they may be clear, and at other points they're more gray in hue. One of the best ways to evaluate your negative thoughts is to go through a systematic list of questions and really tease apart the thought in the moment.

Have a look at the Thought Challenge Questions (Form 11.2). Try to use a rational eye when evaluating you thoughts, and let the Thought Challenge Questions guide you through the process. You can make a copy of the challenge questions, if you like, and carry them around with you. Take some time to go through each question to evaluate your negative thoughts, one at a time, to see if you can chip away at them and develop a more balanced view of the situation, to reduce any associated negative emotions.

Going through the challenge questions one at a time may seem tedious at first, and for many it can be, but the objective is, with practice, to internalize the questions so that after a while you don't need to use the form. The ultimate goal is to be able to recognize, *in your own mind*, when you have a negative automatic thought and to know which questions to use to evaluate it *in that moment*, without ever needing to look at a list or fill out a form.

Let's return again to Judy and her thought: "Ugh. Here we go again. Another night when I'm not going to sleep at all. I'm going to be too tired to be any fun for my kids tomorrow. I won't be fully there for them." Some of the most applicable questions for her thoughts from the Thought Challenge Form are discussed here.

Is There Another Way to Look at This? At 9 p.m., Judy's thought was very black-and-white and catastrophic, assuming a whole night was lost when, in fact, the entire night had not yet even passed. The more she worried about her sleep, the more anxious she would become, making sleep more difficult.

Is There Evidence That This Thought Is True? Yes, Judy was able to note there were nights when she did not sleep all night and was tired the next day. There have been times when she did not feel as fun for the kids and was a lump on the couch at times during the day, not getting everything done that she needed to do.

Is There Evidence Against This Thought? Indeed there is as well. Judy was able to realize that there have been nights where she's had trouble falling asleep but does eventually nod off and struggle with getting up in the morning to her alarm clock. In addition, she noted that there had been times when she slept very poorly but still had a lot of fun with her kids and got everything done the next day that was needed. She was even able to remember a few times when she traveled with her family and didn't sleep well on the flight or in the hotel room while sharing a bed with her snoring husband. Despite the poor sleep during those vacations, she was still able to be engaged and energetic and to enjoy her time with her family. In addition, there had been times when Judy slept very well yet she just felt "off" the next day: lower energy, sleepy, and not as fun all around. The key point here is that sleep is important to our mood and energy, but it isn't always a one-to-one correlation.

Finally, Judy noted that, even if she was extremely tired and sleepy after one of her worst nights, it is highly likely that she could still get out of bed, make simple meals in the microwave for her children, and find activities for them to do to pass the time without needing her constant interaction. Sure, it isn't ideal, but what mom or caretaker hasn't had to struggle with kids at home when she's had the flu or a migraine? Maybe not everything gets done—maybe not even 50 percent gets completed— but it is highly unlikely that after a bad night of sleep there's absolutely no energy to get up and put some milk, cereal, and fruit on the table. Plus, her oldest child is now 9 years old and is likely able to help out more if needed. Judy has wanted to get her to take on more responsibility for her weekly allowance, and this might be a good time to test it out.

What's the Worst Thing That Could Happen If This Thought Were Indeed True? What's the Best Thing? Judy noted that the worst thing she envisioned happening would be that she would not be able to get out of bed and that her children would have to fend for themselves. Judy also saw that she's able to usually catch up on her sleep after a night or two and that, even if she goes without sleep for a night, it is highly likely she'll sleep better the next night or the night after. It is usually temporary. The best thing that would happen with a horrible night is that she would feel fine the next day, there would be no issues with getting out of bed and taking care of her kids, and the next night sleep would come yet again.

What Is the Most Likely Thing to Happen Here? Judy indicated that what would probably happen is what indeed occurs most nights: she would be up for a few hours and then finally fall asleep in the wee hours of the very early morning, only to have her alarm clock wake her up out of her deepest sleep. It was highly likely she'd be tired the next day, but she would get through it, just as she does almost every day of her life. She pushes through, the kids get taken care of, it takes more effort to be fun, but she is able to have a good time with her kids—maybe not 100 percent of the time, but she can string together moments of enjoyment. She also was able to notice that, after pushing for the day, she usually sleeps better the next night, or definitely by the third night in a row, so it is indeed temporary.

Is There Anything I Can Do About This? Judy noted the problem that she often gets into late at night: getting more anxious about sleeping and trying to force sleep to happen. This in turn makes it more difficult for her to fall asleep. Instead, Judy was able to try to take a different approach this time, saying that the more she worries about it, the worse it gets, and there's nothing she can do to force herself to go to sleep—sleep will happen when it happens; worrying about it only makes it harder.

Step 3: Create a Challenge Statement Summary

Now that you've identified your thoughts, written them down, and, for each thought, gone through the Challenge Questions one by one to evaluate them as best you can, it is time to generate a Challenge Statement summary for your Thought Challenge Form. Ideally, this will be a more balanced, rational view of the situation. Synthesize the answers you came up with for the Thought Challenge Questions and come up with a few succinct sentences to "talk back to" the initial negative thoughts and predictions that you wrote down on the form.

Let's get back to Judy's example to highlight how to do this in response to her thought of "Ugh. Here we go again. . . ." Based on her review of the Thought Challenge Questions, she was able to come up with a Challenge

Statement summary: "It isn't even morning yet, and the more I worry about my sleep, the more I won't sleep. I can't force sleep. I might be more tired tomorrow, but I can't necessarily predict this, as there have been days when I've slept poorly and had energy and a good time for my kids. I'll get through the day with my kids and will likely sleep better the next night or the night after."

Form 11.4 shows how Judy filled out the entire form from start to finish. In the last column, after you have come up with the Challenge Statement summary, you will evaluate the effectiveness of the exercise by looking at the outcome. Do you feel less anxious and relaxed? Did it quiet your brain? Do you feel more upset or find that it made you even more frustrated? Judy noted that she felt "much calmer overall."

The goal of cognitive therapy is not to stop these negative thoughts about sleep and daytime functioning from ever happening at all—that is unrealistic. The goal is to *reduce* the emotional reactions and negative behaviors they cause by catching the thoughts faster after they happen, so you can challenge and modify them in the moment. The better you get at doing this, the faster you'll stop the negative spiral that can sometimes happen from negative thoughts about not being about to cope with a bad night of sleep. It is quite possible that, although the thoughts might not completely disappear, you'll have fewer of them as you will get more comfortable with your ability to tolerate a bad night's sleep, and as you have fewer bad nights. In essence, the thoughts might still be there, but there might be fewer of them over time and they might not sting as much when they occur.

PROBLEM SOLVING: COGNITIVE THERAPY

If you find the Thought Challenge Form exercise *doesn't* soften or lighten your emotions, here are some problem-solving issues to consider that might prevent cognitive therapy from working at its best for you.

Should I Challenge a Thought If It Is Actually Completely True?

Definitely not. Cognitive therapy is sometimes misunderstood and described as positive psychology. Thinking positively all the time isn't always beneficial, especially if there's evidence to the contrary. For example, if you genuinely suffer from excessive daytime sleepiness after a poor night's sleep and truly struggle with staying awake throughout the day (although rare, as noted earlier in this book), it is not necessarily helpful to say to yourself, *Everything will be all fine tomorrow. I'll push though and be all good.* It is more helpful in this case to think rationally: know that it is indeed an issue that has evidence behind it, and instead move on to finding a solution to the problem at hand (in this case, managing the daytime sleepiness issues).

I frequently hear women say that they become concerned, in the middle of the night, about getting fired from their jobs if they have a poor night's sleep. For the vast majority of people I've worked with over the years, this thought is highly untrue. However, if there is evidence of a pattern of poor work performance and issues with a boss or clients after a poor night's sleep, simply thinking, *Everything will be fine if I have a bad night's sleep,* is unhelpful. Instead, what's best here is to know that, based on past data, the vast majority of times you've had poor sleep, you've then had issues with a boss or job stability, and you can then be proactive about it. What can be done to prevent getting fired or reprimanded by your boss? Problem solving is important here, as you've identified it as a problem. But, as I said, in the overwhelming majority of Thought Challenge Forms I've seen over the years, most thoughts that insomnia sufferers tend to have about sleep and its negative consequences are quite catastrophic or black-and-white and not 100 percent accurate, usually allowing for room to challenge at least a piece of the thoughts.

What If I Don't Have the Forms on Hand?

The ultimate goal here is to be able to recognize when you have a negative thought that brings down your mood and challenge it *in the moment*, without having to use a formal Thought Challenge Form or the Thought Challenge Questions list. With practice, you should learn to talk back to your thoughts by internalizing the questions discussed in this chapter. And the best way to get to that goal is to practice it in a systematic fashion, going through the forms at first and really looking at the available evidence for and against the thoughts, until the process becomes automatic for you.

Sure, practicality and life sometimes get in the way, and it isn't always possible to say "hold on one minute" while you're in the middle of a work meeting to step to the side and fill out a Thought Challenge Form. The best method at first is to make some copies of the Thought Challenge Form and fill them out for negative thoughts or images about sleep as soon as you have the chance. If it isn't possible to fill out the form in the moment—if you really just don't have any time whatsoever—try to jot down on your phone, on a piece of paper, a napkin, wherever you can, any thoughts as they pop up in the moment. The faster you get them down, the clearer they'll be. Then fill out the form later as best you can. To help you in the process, use your smartphone to take a picture of the form and the list of Thought Challenge Questions so you can review them on short notice.

I Completed a Thought Challenge Form for a Negative Thought, and It Didn't Change My Mood at All!

Sometimes, if you're not noticing any change after evaluating your negative automatic thoughts, make sure you've gotten to the root of the thought. When we write them down or say them out loud, we tend to somewhat rationalize our thoughts and temper them more than what may actually be in our head. It is really important to get to the core thought(s) that's keeping you up or making you worried about your sleep or the consequences of a lack of sleep. Also, it is important that you truly believe the thought challenge statement you come up with. When someone just goes through the motions and questions a negative thought but does not really internalize or truly believe the evidence against the thought (or whatever challenge questions are used), shifting the thought into more neutral territory becomes much more difficult.

Finally, if you still struggle with the same thoughts over and over again, and despite challenging them they keep coming back or they don't decrease in severity, you might find mindfulness (discussed in Chapter 12) to be more useful overall. With practice, mindfulness helps you notice the thoughts when they occur but let them pass and not grab onto them (which then leads to the anxiety cycle before bed).

Do I Have to Keep Doing a Thought Challenge Form Even If I Have the Same Thoughts Time After Time?

It is quite likely that you will start to see the same thoughts or themes pop up over and over again, especially when related to your sleep. For example, you might see that when you awaken early in the morning you often have a thought, *I won't be able to get through work today*. After a number of times evaluating the thought and coming up with a challenge statement, you'll have a good sense of how to challenge that thought without even needing to write it down.

A helpful strategy here is to complete a "coping card." For example, if you notice that you frequently have a thought, *I never get anything done because of poor sleep*, and find that you're frequently challenging this thought night after night and day after day, you can make a coping card to make challenging that easier. On one side of a blank index card, write down the automatic thought—the thought that tends to be increasing your frustration, anxiety, and worry—just as you would on a Thought

Challenge Form. Now, turn the coping card over and write your usual Challenge Statement Summary, one that lowers your anxiety, stress, sadness, or frustration. Then, when you have that thought again, you can simply use the coping card rather than going through the typical motions of taking out a Thought Challenge Form and questioning everything to get at the same conclusion as usual. Instead, you have it right at your fingertips. I find this strategy particularly helpful for women begin to worry as bedtime gets closer and some of those "here we go again" thoughts come up. Have a few coping cards next to your bed will help bring your tired mind into a more rational state.

Takeaway Message: Cognitive Therapy

✓ Our thoughts can be our biggest sleep stealers.

✓ Worries about (not) getting enough sleep or daytime consequences of poor sleep and trying to force sleep to happen only make us more frustrated, tense, and anxious, thereby making sleep even harder to obtain.

✓ The Thought Challenge Form (Form 11.1) and Thought Challenge Questions (Form 11.2) are additional tools to evaluate your worries, generating alternative ways to view your thoughts. and quiet your brain.

FORM 11.1: **Thought Challenge Form**

Directions: When you notice your mood getting worse (anxious, sad, worried), ask yourself, *What am I thinking right now?* Record the thought *as soon as possible* in the "Negative Thoughts and Predictions" column. Then fill out the rest of the form and consider how accurate or realistic the thoughts may be.

Date and Time	Situation	Mood	Negative Thoughts and Predictions	Challenge Statement(s)	Outcome
	Where are (were) you?	*What emotions are you feeling?*	*What thought just went through your mind? Also consider any images/pictures you may have had in your mind at the time.*	*Using the questions on Form 11.2 to challenge your thoughts, try to generate a more balanced response to the negative thoughts.*	*What emotions are you experiencing now? Are they as strong as before?*

FORM 11.2: **Thought Challenge Questions**

Use these questions to challenge the negative thoughts and predictions that you enter on the Thought Challenge Form (Form 11.1).

1. Is there another way to look at this? Think of all the alternatives (for example, *My boss may have not called me back because she has been busy with her own family and work stressors*).

2. Is there evidence that this thought is true? (for example, *I had a few select days when I though it was harder to think off the top of my head, or I sometimes find my morning runs to be more of a challenge when I haven't slept well*).

3. Is there evidence against this thought? (for example, *I've never been reprimanded at work after a poor night's sleep; in fact I've been complimented on a presentation after only 3 hours of sleep*).

4. What's the worst thing that could happen if this thought were indeed true? What's the best thing? (for example, *Worst possible: I could lose my job and have to downsize my house. Best possible: I could get a promotion*).

5. What is the most likely thing to happen here? (for example, *Nothing good or bad. I'll continue in my job as I've been doing and all will remain fine regardless of how much sleep I've gotten*).

6. Is there anything I can do about this? (for example, *Get out of bed if I'm tossing and turning and do something quiet, calm, and relaxing in dim light to pass the time. Continuing to worry about poor sleep impacting my job with no evidence behind it is only going to make me sleep less*).

FORM 11.3: Judy's Thought Challenge Form—Step 1, Noting Negative Thoughts and Predictions

Directions: When you notice your mood getting worse (anxious, sad, worried), ask yourself, *What am I thinking right now?* Record the thought *as soon as possible* in the "Negative Thoughts and Predictions" column. Then fill out the rest of the form and consider how accurate or realistic the thoughts may be.

Date and Time	Situation	Mood	Negative Thoughts and Predictions	Challenge Statement(s)	Outcome
	Where are (were) you?	*What emotions are you feeling?*	*What thought just went through your mind? Also consider any images/pictures you may have had in your mind at the time.*	*Using the questions on Form 11.2 to challenge your thoughts, try to generate a more balanced response to the negative thoughts.*	*What emotions are you experiencing now? Are they as strong as before?*
9/4/17 9:00 pm	*Doing the dishes and feeling energetic*	*Anxious, frustrated*	*Ugh. Here I am yet again, another night when I'm not going to sleep.* *I'm going to be too tired to be any fun for my kids tomorrow. I won't be able to fully be there for them.*		

FORM 11.4: Judy's Completed Thought Challenge Form

Directions: When you notice your mood getting worse (anxious, sad, worried), ask yourself, *What am I thinking right now?* Record the thought *as soon as possible* in the "Negative Thoughts and Predictions" column. Then fill out the rest of the form and consider how accurate or realistic the thoughts may be.

Date and Time	Situation	Mood	Negative Thoughts and Predictions	Challenge Statement(s)	Outcome
	Where are (were) you?	*What emotions are you feeling?*	*What thought just went through your mind? Also consider any images/pictures you may have had in your mind at the time.*	*Using the questions on Form 11.2 to challenge your thoughts, try to generate a more balanced response to the negative thoughts.*	*What emotions are you experiencing now? Are they as strong as before?*
9/4/17 9:00 pm	*Doing the dishes and feeling energetic*	*Anxious, frustrated*	*Ugh. Here I am yet again, another night when I'm not going to sleep.* *I'm going to be too tired to be any fun for my kids tomorrow. I won't be able to fully be there for them.*	*It isn't even morning yet, and the more I worry about my sleep, the more I won't sleep. I can't force sleep. I might be more tired tomorrow, but I can't necessarily predict this, as there have been days when I've slept poorly and had energy and a good time for my kids. I'll get through the day with my kids and will likely sleep better the next night or the night after.*	*Much calmer overall.*

12.

Tips for Productive and Unproductive Worries

Here's another little test for you. Don't think about it, don't. *Don't think about this.* There's a big, pink elephant (don't think about it) in a tutu—don't think about it. He's over in the corner, spinning around in circles and eating a sandwich. *Don't think about it.*

Now, stop and think: what's the first thing that comes to your mind, this instant? If you're like every other person I've given this little quiz to over the years, you're probably thinking about a silly pink elephant in the corner, spinning around and eating a sandwich. No matter how hard you tell yourself not to think about it and suppress the image, you simply cannot stop yourself from thinking about it. But that's totally OK! You're human, and this is typical human behavior. The more we tell ourselves *not* to do something, the more we start to do or think about it.

This exercise is a relatively easy way to demonstrate how thought suppression only leads to thoughts coming back stronger and stronger: it simply isn't a good strategy to try to ignore our thoughts and worries. Instead, "worry time," initially developed for people with generalized anxiety disorder, is a relatively simple strategy that has been demonstrated to reduce chronic worry in many women with insomnia. Women in general tend to have busier brains overall, with more mental chatter compared to men. Add to that a layer of insomnia and/or anxiety, if it exists, and the daily/hourly/minute-by-minute concerns and worries about anything and everything—from *Did I put my son into the right summer camp this year* to *I don't have any groceries for dinner* and *I didn't sleep last night, and I can't bear another lost night of sleep*—can feel like a hamster wheel, never ending and always going around and around in a circle. It is exhausting, physically and mentally.

The reason this ties in so nicely with the pink elephant example is that the more often you go to bed at night and try to tell yourself not to worry about or not think about something, trying to suppress the thoughts, the more and more they start popping up throughout the night and during the daytime. I think of it like the whack-a-mole game at a carnival: the more you whack away a thought or worry, trying to ignore it, the faster another one will pop up . . . and another one, and another one.

WORRY TIME: AN EFFECTIVE TOOL FOR UNPRODUCTIVE WORRY

Worry time changes that paradigm altogether. Instead of thinking, *I'm going to ignore this concern/worry,* you acknowledge its existence with open arms—at the proper time. Instead of trying not to think it, you see the thought, you make note of it, and you say to yourself, *I hear you, but I'm going to think about you during my set-aside worry time.* This way, you're giving the worries their due attention, but at the same time you're also not allowing yourself to think unproductively at varying times throughout the day and night (cue the hamster wheel again).

When we just worry for the sake of worrying but don't actually come to a conclusion or even a tiny next step to move us toward an eventual outcome, the worries serve little purpose besides creating unnecessary mental chatter, increased anxiety, and poor sleep. This unproductive worry is the ultimate target of worry time. In worry time, you quickly notice the worries, even the unproductive ones, but you come up with a way to worry in a more controlled manner, not 24/7.

The instructions for doing worry time are quite simple in theory but require some practice. Patience and consistency are needed with this technique because you're adopting a new habit and getting rid of an old one, and that takes time.

1. *Set aside 20 minutes each day as your designated worry time.* I don't advise you do it immediately before bed every night, but many of the women I've worked with find it helpful to do about 2–3 hours before bedtime. Find a time that works for you, one that you can stick with.

2. *Find a comfortable spot at a table.* Have a blank piece of paper and a pen in front of you and get comfortable.

3. *Use a timer.* Set a timer for 20 minutes, no more, no less.

4. GO! Worry the heck out of *everything* you've been worrying about—miniscule or huge. Write it all down, free from answers, judgments, conclusions, and so on. Just write down the worries. For example, "I'll never get good sleep again." "I'll never find a job I love." "Did I remember to pick up the dry cleaning?" "I don't have time to clean the house before my parents arrive for the week!" Don't judge yourself and don't stop—just write.

5. *Keep going!* A common conundrum with worry time is that women often feel that they're constantly worried, but when worry time comes around they struggle to fill the 20 minutes with worries. This is usually because the worries of the day are often of the same theme, popping up over and over, asking to be recognized but with no answer in sight. If you think you're done worrying and the timer hasn't gone off yet for 20 minutes, go back to worrying again about the same things. Again, worry the heck out of them—and if you worry about not worrying enough (or too much) or not doing worry time properly, write it down!

6. *Walk away at 20 minutes and throw away the paper.* Once the timer goes off, you're done. Throw away the paper—it serves no purpose other than to help you get out all of your worries.

7. *"Not now, during worry time."* Here's the real star of this treatment technique and, admittedly, the toughest part to follow. You're going to worry during the day—that's OK. The difference now, though, is that when you notice a worry start up—whatever it may be, small or big—acknowledge the thought and say to yourself, *I see you, but I'm not going to think about you now. I'll think about you during worry time.* Here, you're allowing yourself to notice and acknowledge the thought, but you are not rehashing it over and over. You're going to think about it during worry time. You will have to do this over and over again at first, as you gradually train your brain not to worry constantly.

Worry time is not a time for productive worry or coming to conclusions on things. It is a time to notice your worries, think about why they're bothering you so much, and write them down. It is *not* a time to challenge them using cognitive therapy or problem solving. Again, be patient and consistent in your practice with worry time, if you think that this might be a useful technique and give it a try.

WORRY PRODUCTIVELY WITH TO-DO LISTS

Sometimes our worries about poor sleep and daily issues with family, children, money, and job are there for some good reason, to motivate us to come to a solution or answer to the problem. The anxiety is a signal to fight the issue at hand and come up with a solution. This is known as *productive worry.* The worry needs to be addressed, for good reason—if it doesn't get taken care of, it'll spin around and around until you do something about it.

For some women, just doing worry time can be too overwhelming because no solutions are generated. If you find that you need to be more constructive in your worry, try productive worrying instead. This technique is particularly helpful for women who wake up in the middle of the night thinking of the things that need to be done, concerned they'll forget about them or about how to take care of them. If you practice productive worrying well before bedtime, you can gently remind yourself in the middle of the night that you've already written down a next step to take care of the issue and that you won't forget about it because it is documented and being addressed during the daytime hours.

1. Take a piece of blank paper and draw a line down the middle. On the left side write "To Do," and on the right side write "Next Step." Start this in the evening, about 2–3 hours before bedtime. Set a timer for 20 minutes; stop at the end of the 20 minutes.

2. In the "To Do" column, write down the things that need to be done or things you are worrying about and that need to be figured out in a constructive, productive way. For example, "I have to make all the lunches for my kids this week and I have no time to get to the market." "The sink is full of dishes." "Carolyn is mad at me because of what I said to her at work, and I think she might be right." It can truly be anything.

3. In the "Next Step" column, you don't need to write the ultimate solution (such as fixing your relationship with Carolyn, which might not be so simple). Instead, just focus on one *next* thing you can do so you move closer to an ultimate solution. Sometimes, the solution is just "Go to the market tomorrow just before work and get food for lunch." Sometimes it is more complicated, like "I don't have time to get to the market. I'll ask my partner to go on the way home from work to pick up some bread, bananas, and peanut butter."

4. Put the form somewhere in your room near your bed. This way, when you awaken at night, you can remind yourself that you've written it down and have a next step written down.

Takeaway Message: Worry Better

✓ Two ways to dial down the volume of our worries are practicing worry time and productive worrying.
✓ Confront unproductive worries using worry time.
✓ Tackle productive worries in a systematic fashion with a to-do list.

13.

Mindfulness

⁓

Research has demonstrated that women's brains are set up to multitask more than men's. Offer and Schneider (2011) found that, even when faced with comparable workloads, mothers tend to feel more burdened and stressed than fathers. In fact, their research suggested that, compared to their male counterparts at home, mothers spent on average 10 more hours per week multitasking on tasks such as housework and childcare. This multitasking for women was frequently associated with increased stress, poorer quality of life, negative emotion, and increased conflict at work and home.

Women tend to pride themselves on multitasking, as we think it makes us more efficient and better at juggling all that goes on in our daily life. The reality is that this couldn't be further from the truth. Although we may likely be better than men at multitasking, and do it significantly more often than men, multitasking negatively affects performance. We are less productive when switching back and forth between tasks, and we have trouble remembering what needs to be done. Multitasking makes us more distractible, making it far more challenging to focus on something from start to finish due to a diminished ability to sustain attention.

Women are also more prone to worry and are twice as likely to suffer from an anxiety disorder than are men. We tend to spend a significant amount of time thinking or worrying about the future—what needs to be done, what could happen, what shouldn't happen—and spending much less time being in the present moment. Men do not have these same tendencies overall.

Traditional CBT-I focuses on stimulus control, sleep restriction, sleep hygiene, and cognitive therapy. As I hope you understand by now, cognitive therapy is great for some women, helping them to realistically evaluate negative thoughts about poor sleep and its effects during the daytime.

Even though cognitive therapy has its place for a good deal of women, a sleepy and/or super busy brain is not always a rational brain, and it is often quite difficult for some people to evaluate their negative automatic thoughts in a judgment-free, balanced manner. I've worked with women over the years who have consistently challenged their negative thoughts about sleep and generated rational responses on coping cards, but the same worries keep popping up again, and again, and again (like that whack-a-mole at the carnival again). Each time the thought pops up, you're hitting it down using cognitive therapy techniques, but it just isn't enough, and they keep popping up, faster and faster.

The busy brain is filled with thoughts about sleep, daytime, what needs to be done in order to sleep, and what doesn't get done if sleep is missed. You might be tired, but your brain is going and going and *just won't shut off.* Sometimes there's no anxious thought process; your brain simply has a constant narrative about all of the day's events and what is coming up in the future. It is almost like the brain's volume is set to 14 on a dial that ends at a 10. This mental state is commonly described as *tired but wired.*

In some circumstances, finding a way to intervene with cognitive therapy in these cases can be downright exhausting and might not always be fruitful since you are constantly interrupting the persistent narrative of thoughts in order to challenge them. My colleague Dr. Jason Ong has dedicated much of his career to developing a newer way to address the busy mind during insomnia, and he has done so by introducing mindfulness.

Some people think mindfulness may merely be the next hot topic in psychology and that this too shall pass. Although it has gotten a lot of press in the past, mindfulness should be here to stay, given how much benefit it brings to those who practice it on a regular basis. Originating nearly 2,500 years ago and rooted in Buddhist traditions, mindfulness is a way to cultivate a calm body and mind through the act of paying attention to the present moment in a nonjudgmental way.

Jon Kabat-Zinn created the first mindfulness-based stress reduction program over 20 years ago, and it has proven quite successful for lowering anxiety and stress in many patients (Kabat-Zinn, 2013). Mindfulness-based programs have been successfully adapted to a wide array of problems, including stress and anxiety, chronic pain, depression, and addiction. Although utilizing mindfulness as a treatment component in traditional CBT-I is still relatively new overall, a good deal of promising research supports its use (Black O'Reilly, Olmstead, Breen & Irwin, 2015; Ong et al., 2014; Ong, Shapiro, & Manber, 2009; Ong & Sholtes, 2010; Shapiro, Bootzin, Figueredo, Lopez & Schwartz, 2003), and I frequently use it with my patients with good benefit. Mindfulness for insomnia targets the busy brain, physical arousal (anxious feelings), and the hyperfocus on sleep and its consequences.

I routinely practice mindfulness myself, and I encourage everyone to do the same. We are busy—too busy—and our female brains are programmed to think about a million things at once. Mindfulness brings me into the present moment, helps me figure out what needs to get done right here and now, and gives me a much needed snap back into reality outside of my head.

Mindfulness is simply the act of focusing on the present moment, on what is in front of you. It is often made into a more complicated issue than it really needs be. One of the simplest mindfulness exercises is to just sit in a chair for 30 seconds and notice what's going on around you. Do you hear anything? Smell anything? What exactly do you see? Describe the textures, colors that are in front of you. Is your mind wandering to something else? If so, notice those thoughts and, without judgment, bring your attention back to the present moment of noticing what is in the here and now.

Many women struggle with the aspect of judgment during a mindfulness practice. There is no one right way to do it, aside from being in the present moment and bringing your thoughts back to the present moment when they wander. I've been guilty of this on far too many occasions: I'll be completing a mindfulness exercise, and throughout the entire practice, my mind will wander to such thoughts as *This is stupid, this will never help me find some calm*, or *I forgot to pick up the dry cleaning*, or *I didn't pack a snack for my son's lunch*. I'll then refocus to the mindfulness exercise at hand, but the judgment sets in when my mind wanders: *Why can't I stick with the same exercise for 30 seconds and focus the entire time? I should be able to focus!* The key in any mindfulness exercise is not to keep a razor-sharp focus on the present moment the entire time. The skill is in being able to refocus your brain on the present moment when it goes off.

Mindfulness is essentially a mental muscle that needs to be strengthened through practice. The more you do it, the easier it becomes. However, even if you're strong, there will still be days that are a challenge. It is particularly useful for insomnia work because it allows you to notice your busy mind—whether it is full of thoughts about sleep, life, or just what color to paint your living room, notice that the thoughts are there but then let them go without getting caught up in the stream. It is very difficult to just "be mindful" at all times. Aim for just a few seconds of mindfulness at a time, working your way up to 5 minutes or more. With practice comes more ability to use it in more challenging, varied, and/or stressful circumstances.

A former mentor of mine once likened our thoughts and mindfulness to a luggage carousel at the airport. You get off your plane and go to baggage claim, only to stand there for a while and watch as all of the luggage goes around and around on the carousel in front of you. Each piece of luggage is a separate thought. Some thoughts are benign, and some are maybe more emotionally challenging. Most insomnia patients with over-active minds tend to grab onto each piece of luggage as it comes off the conveyor belt. Before you know it, you're loaded with way too much bag-gage and can't handle everything that's coming your way. Instead, mind-fulness teaches us to notice each piece of luggage as a separate, distinct piece. We notice what it looks like, how it might make us think or feel, how heavy it is. Instead of picking up each suitcase, we see it for what it is and then let every piece of luggage pass by on the conveyor belt. We see it, acknowledge it, but don't pick it up.

I find it quite fascinating, but I often notice that women's lives start to improve when their thoughts about sleep shift—even if their sleep doesn't necessarily change right away. Once the busy brain and wor-ries about sleep start to calm down and the patient doesn't hang onto thoughts about sleep, better sleep starts to happen. Dr. Ong's work has demonstrated that consistent and daily daytime mindfulness practice (even as short as a few minutes each day!) can strengthen the mindful brain, allowing us to notice when noisy thoughts begin to interfere with sleep and then let them go (as opposed to getting stuck on them).

The point of a mindfulness exercise is to bring awareness to your thoughts in order to let them go. It is *not* meant to be a sedative. I've certainly worked with many women over the years who swear by these exercises in bed for sleep, but the overall goal is to practice these exercises during the daytime or wind-down routine to bring a sense of awareness to the moment, letting go of a busy mind. Many apps are available for smartphones that have mindfulness meditations exercises on them. You should ideally not be reliant on them to fall asleep every night. What would happen if the phone lost charge or the app stopped working? You might not be able to sleep out of dependence on the app to do so! The apps are ideal to help you cultivate a mindfulness practice and I highly recommend using them anytime during the day or during a wind-down practice, but try to avoid using them in bed as your nightly sedative.

Mindfulness is not specifically an exercise to relax you, though that may happen as a bonus. Instead, mindfulness is just about noticing your noisy (or even quiet!) brain, noticing the thoughts come and go (not simply just pushing them out) and observing them from afar without getting tangled up in them.

Bringing conscious awareness to your eating is a simple, portable way to practice mindfulness. We are often rushing through life and don't focus on eating. Sometimes, we're feeding our kids and running around to make lunches or do the dishes while taking a few bites of the leftover food now and then; other times we might be sitting at the table across from a loved one with the TV on or our cell phones in our hands as we consume our dinner.

To practice mindfulness with your eating, sit down at the table in front of your food. Notice the color, texture, shape, and smell. Simply observe. Once you take your first bite, notice where in your mouth the food is now located. What do you taste? Smell? What textures do you feel? Silently labeling each observation, such as smooth, sweet, or crunchy, can help ground you and keep you in the present. If your mind wanders off task, simply notice you wandered and nonjudgmentally get back on track.

There are endless ways to practice mindfulness at home or on the go. You might come across apps, recordings, or books that focus on mindfulness meditation. Although it can be confusing at times, I like to think of mindfulness as a skill that you're practicing, and I think of meditation as a more formalized way of practicing the skill. Dozens, if not hundreds, of apps for smartphones, both paid and free, are available with guided mindfulness exercises. Some exercises have you focus on your thoughts or certain images; others, on relaxing your muscles or your breath.

I try to practice mindfulness in little pockets throughout the day. Whenever I'm able to get a manicure, I make a conscious effort to be mindful during the hand massage. I notice the pressure of the massage, the feel of the lotion, and how tense or relaxed my hands and shoulders are during the exercise. I also like to practice mindfulness when I do the dishes after my children are done with dinner and playing with my husband. I take a chore that I typically dislike (such as cleaning dishes) and work on noticing the negative thoughts I'm having about the task and then practice letting them pass. I instead focus my mind solely on the feel of the warm water on my skin and the look of the bubbles in the water.

Adding a mindfulness exercise into your nightly wind-down routine can help calm the mind and body as well. Listen to music mindfully while in your wind-down chair. I often try to focus on the various textures in the music I might be listening to before bed, with a particular emphasis on following the bass line for a minute or two. Other times I might try to pay specific attention to the intricacy of a piano part, or the tone of a vocalist's voice without trying to interpret lyrics. I also make my nighttime face-washing routine into a quick mindfulness exercise by noticing the varying sensations of my facial products (such as the tingling of the under-eye gel, the soothing feel of my toner, the silky texture of the moisturizer).

A morning mindfulness practice can be really helpful as well. Often a busy day is ahead of us, and we struggle to get a grip on our immediately racing thoughts upon awakening. Keeping a routine morning mindfulness practice can help awaken the brain and bring stability and focus to your morning. You may even find that, with regular practice, you begin to enjoy awakening just for the moments of quiet that mindfulness brings as you start your day.

Try this mindfulness exercise in the morning: When you first wake up, go stand by the window. Open up the shades and just observe and describe what you see. Is it cloudy? Is it sunny? Rainy? Note the color of the sky, the shape of the clouds. Is it still dark outside? Is the sun just now coming up? If you find your mind wandering to something else—like how you are still sleepy and want to get back to bed, or how you don't want to deal with all that the day has ahead—gently refocus your thoughts back on describing what you see out the window. Note any judgments about the current weather (such as *Another rainy day!* Or *It's so cold out, I don't want to leave the house!*), and practice refocusing on just observing what you see in front of you. Feel your breath as you inhale and exhale. Move your focus to your feet on the floor. See how firmly you are standing there; notice the different textures below your feet and the temperature of the floor. Now stretch your arms out, open your eyes nice and wide, and begin your day.

As another mindfulness exercise, take a break right now from reading this book and set a timer for 1 minute to practice being mindful by sitting quietly and observing the noises in the room around you. Ideally, with daily practice (regardless of the time you work on it), you'll notice your mental chatter decrease, become more aware of negative sleep talk (e.g. "I'll never fall asleep tonight" or "I need to sleep tonight or else X, Y, Z will happen") and you'll find you fall asleep faster.

Takeaway Message: Mindfulness

✓ While women may multitask more than, and somewhat better than, men do, we also have busier and more anxious brains overall.

✓ Despite popular belief, multitasking is not as efficient or effective as performing one task at a time.

✓ Our brains typically have a lot of mental chatter, and women with insomnia tend to have lots of mental noise related to sleep, worries about sleep, and what will happen as a result of poor sleep.

✓ Cultivating a practice of mindfulness on a regular basis has been shown to help us quiet our brain and observe noisy thoughts without getting stuck on them.

✓ Allowing ourselves to not get stuck on nighttime thoughts, and instead to let them pass by, quiets the brain at night and sets a much better stage for sleep.

PART 4

Beyond Cognitive Behavioral Therapy for Insomnia

14.

What If CBT-I Isn't Enough?

DR. KATHERINE TAKAYASU*

What do you do when you've made a lot of behavioral and cognitive changes in earnest, but it just isn't enough? Well, it's time to think of complementary strategies.

Integrative medicine is a field that bridges mainstream medicine with evidence-based complementary medicine. In integrative medicine we think about lifestyle as the fertile ground in which the seeds of psychotherapy, medications, herbs, supplements, and acupuncture are sown. Just imagine trying to plant a flower in a barren field where the soil has been stripped of nutrients. Obviously, it wouldn't thrive. Your lifestyle choices—how you eat, how you move, how you attend to your inner self, in addition to how you sleep—are choices that can fertilize your soil and make the seeds of CBT-I grow. First things first: let's discuss your lifestyle.

---

* Katherine Wehri Takayasu, M.D., M.B.A., practices Integrative Medicine at Stamford Hospital in Connecticut, where she helps patients heal naturally with acupuncture, mind-body medicine, botanicals, nutrition, and lifestyle optimization. She's an Assistant Professor of Clinical Medicine at Columbia University/New York Presbyterian.

LIFESTYLE OPTIMIZATION

Lifestyle includes what I call the "3+1": the three necessary things we do on a daily basis are eating, moving, and sleeping, and the "+1" denotes being mindful of spiritual needs. The American way of life is jam-packed. We've found a way to take the pleasures of life and compact them into tiny bites. Don't have time to cook? Eat this sodium-laden, frozen, processed, but totally organic and wholesome meal that you don't have to lift a finger for. (Sense my sarcasm?) Don't have time to exercise? Sweat bullets with a high-intensity interval-training workout for 8 minutes and rev up your stress response rather than soothe your soul. Don't have time to meditate? Play with your smartphone while lying on the acupuncture table trying to alleviate your back pain and anxiety problems. (More than I would like to admit, I catch patients on the acupuncture table with needles in their hands trying to answer text messages!)

Why are your nutrition, exercise, and meditation habits meaningful to sleep? Consider that people who optimize their lifestyles generally enjoy more restorative sleep. Numerous studies show positive associations between lifestyle optimization and sleep, but it's hard to know which is the chicken and which is the egg. In other words, we don't have clear data on whether good nutrition, moderate exercise, and meditation practice lead to better sleep, or if good sleep helps set the stage for being able to follow through with good lifestyle practices. If you want to sleep better, it makes sense to get your lifestyle habits on track.

Eating and Drinking

Let's start with food. What kind of nutrition plan is optimal? The best piece of advice comes from whole food activist and best-selling author Michael Pollan (2008): "Eat food. Not too much. Mostly plants." Sounds simple, right? It actually *is* simple, but most of us get sidetracked by low-fat this and low-carb that, confusing what should be an easy answer.

It is a good idea not to follow one specific way of eating but to look at where all reasonable diets overlap. These areas of overlap suggest the correct way to eat includes vegetables, fruit, plant-based protein, high-quality animal protein, monounsaturated fats, whole grains, omega-3-rich foods, and fermented foods. Now, of course, there are some idiosyncrasies based on your personal constitution. Not everyone is made to eat every food. Do cruciferous vegetables like broccoli or cauliflower give you terrible gas no matter how you prepare them? Well, then, maybe those aren't the best choices for you. But good news: there are a lot of other delicious vegetables out there for you to enjoy!

Another important lifestyle factor is being mindful about caffeine and alcohol. You can feel comfortable having one or two cups of coffee in the morning, as evidence supports the connection between cognitive function and a modest amount of caffeine. Caffeine should be limited to morning hours. Caffeine can be measured in the bloodstream up to 12 hours after it's consumed and may interfere with sleep. Likewise, for alcohol the best advice for women is from my favorite cardiologist: "Ladies, it's one drink a day, and you can't save it up!" I encourage patients to keep alcohol consumption to three or four days a week and only one drink each day for women and two drinks each day for men. Unfortunately, our bodies are not adept at detoxing more alcohol than that. As explained earlier, alcohol inhibits our ability to enter the deep, restorative sleep that our body needs to repair itself during the night.

Moving

The second component of the fertile ground is exercise—this is my favorite feel-good pill. I tell patients the number one reason to exercise is the production of feel-good hormones called endorphins. A randomized controlled trial published in 1999 in the *Archives of Internal Medicine* compared moderate exercise to SSRIs (selective serotonin reuptake inhibitors), the standard treatment of depression and anxiety (Blumenthal et al., 1999). And you know what? Patients who exercised three times each week had the same improvement in their mental health as those who took medications. This finding was further strengthened by a 2006 meta-analysis that combined data from 11 different randomized controlled trials (Stathopoulou, Powers, Berry, Smits & Otto, 2006).

There's also extensive research to show that exercise influences our sleep and regulates our circadian rhythms. Much of the sleep research suggests that exercising around 4–6 hours before bedtime might be the best for those with insomnia, but this recommendation may not be conducive to your lifestyle. If you are a "morning person," then you may benefit from getting your motor started each day with a morning walk.

Mindfulness

The "+1" component of the fertile ground of lifestyle is attending to the mind-body connection. Our brains have the beautiful capacity to remodel over time, called *neuroplasticity*. This ability means that practicing relaxation techniques helps us relax more and more over time. Neuroscientists like to say, "Neurons that fire together, wire together." You know neuroplasticity in your own life as the ability to learn lyrics to a song after hearing it on the radio a few times. The brain-body connection is strong, and attending to a mind-body practice on a daily basis can change your brain and body over time to react more calmly. It's important to engage in regular practice. Just like we don't expect completely toned muscles if we go to the gym just once to do bicep curls, our relaxation response requires gentle attention each day to develop a better and better response over time. I started meditating when my twin boys were a few months old. I was past the phase of utter exhaustion, so intermittent awakenings during the night would keep me awake long after the boys got back to sleep. I think it took me a few months before I really garnered the benefit of simple breathing exercises and progress. Sometimes it's hard to be that patient, but you've chosen to read this book because you value a nonpharmaceutical approach—it took time for you to develop your insomnia, and it will take time to train yourself out of it.

I encourage you to choose any form of meditation that feels good to you. In addition to mindfulness practice, try your hand at various breathing exercises, progressive muscle relaxation, guided imagery, or even a movement-based meditation like yoga, tai chi, or qigong. Make a commitment to try it daily for 3 weeks (research shows there's something very special about that 21-day mark!), and then see how you feel. Look at all areas of your life—your sleep, concentration, energy, irritability—and determine if you're a little better off than before. But also cut yourself some slack, and know that it could take longer to get into a mindful state. I tried yoga for a whole year before I understood the concept of Savasana, the pose of complete relaxation, which involves simply laying on the yoga map, completely still. At first I thought Savasana was a waste of time and suitable only for making a to-do list for the rest of the day, but now it's my favorite pose! Imagine knowing that your only purpose in a moment is to lie on your mat and relax. That's bliss!

This was a quick review of how your lifestyle can build fertile soil for CBT-I to better help you with insomnia. Obviously, none of these interventions is the silver bullet. I coach patients to understand, however, that all these tiny changes end up bringing about meaningful change.

AN INTEGRATIVE APPROACH TO INSOMNIA

Now let's move on to discussing an integrative approach to several conditions that might be affecting your sleep. We'll start with strategies to manage insomnia without any associated issue (medical or psychiatric), and then move on to managing associated conditions like anxiety, depression, and chronic pain, and then finally round out with strategies to cope with perimenopausal sleep issues.

Integrative management needs the fertile ground of a balanced life-style, so you can't just skip over the nutrition, exercise, and mind-body parts and move onto a botanical or pharmaceutical approaches to sleep, because these don't work very well on their own. Each topic that follows include the use of botanicals and supplements, traditional pharmaceutical management, and applicable complementary treatments like acupuncture.

Note: CBT-I is the first-line treatment for most people with insomnia. If you need to move on to any of the alternative strategies discussed below, this chapter is meant to stimulate a conversation with your doctor about your specific situation. You should discuss treatment options with your doctor before starting anything on your own, as even over-the-counter supplements may have interactions with any medications you may be taking. It is best to have a thoughtful discussion with your physician regarding these options and to weigh the costs (such as potential side effects, interactions with other medications) and benefits (ideally improved sleep) of adding something into your sleep program if truly necessary.

Insomnia Without Any Associated Issues

For people who have insomnia without any co-occurring issues like depression or anxiety, a variety of options are available to add if CBT-I alone is not working well enough. These generally fall into three categories: herbs and supplements, over-the-counter and prescribed pharmaceuticals, and acupuncture.

Herbs and Supplements. Almost everyone who has struggled with sleep has tried melatonin. This is actually a natural hormone made by the pineal gland in our brain as a response to darkness. There are several natural ways to increase your own melatonin production, including avoiding blue-light technology at night and decreasing the body temperature. The most relaxing way to alter the body temperature is with a hot bath or hot shower about 90 minutes before bed. Melatonin is released once your body temperature begins to cool off. Many substances blunt your natural melatonin release, like caffeine, nicotine, alcohol, some blood pressure medications, and over-the-counter analgesics. Although many women use melatonin for insomnia, it is actually most beneficial for those who suffer from jet lag and night owl syndrome when taken in very low doses (0.3–1 mg) *many* hours before bedtime. Surprisingly to some, research results are mixed on the use of melatonin for insomnia. For those who find it helpful for sleep, 3–5 mg maximum taken approximately an hour before bed is the standard (you'll see much higher doses in the pharmacy, and that is frequently when worsened side effects tend to occur). A huge problem with melatonin is the dose from bottle to bottle and from company to company, as many supplement doses are too strong, and as a dietary supplement, it is not currently regulated by the FDA. The most common side effects are nausea, dizziness, headache, irritability, and daytime drowsiness. Also, remember that melatonin is naturally made in your brain. By taking melatonin supplements for a prolonged time, your brain will begin to rely on the supplements more and more, thereby producing less melatonin naturally. So while it might help you from time to time (and even then it isn't a panacea for most people), over time your brain might get to accustomed to it and not produce melatonin on its own.

Magnesium is a natural element found in the body and involved in several body functions. This supplement can be helpful for a variety of conditions aside from sleep, including headaches, menstrual-related cramping, restless legs, muscle cramps, constipation, and general anxiety or stress. Magnesium allows the nervous system to relax, which is quite helpful right before sleep, and many women tend to be somewhat magnesium deficient. Magnesium is available in the diet in the form of leafy greens (another reason to eat kale!), nuts, seeds, and a variety of other healthy foods. Supplementation can be tricky, as the type of magnesium salt can change its effects on the body, specifically in the digestive system. If you tend toward constipation, then a bit of magnesium citrate or oxide can be helpful; otherwise, choose magnesium glycinate. Doses of around 400 mg at night are standard, but there is some range with this, and a discussion with your doctor may be helpful to determine the optimal amount. Magnesium is safe for pregnant and lactating women. You can also consider massaging magnesium oil into your skin or bathing in magnesium salts (like Epsom salts) for alternative forms of absorption.

Valerian is another common herb used for sleep, though yet again with very limited data behind its use—even less than melatonin. As with other sleep herbs, it should be used only in the short term. It can also be consumed as a tea and promotes relaxation. One catch is that it requires 2–3 weeks of nightly use before seeing a positive effect. Typical dosing is 800–1200 mg of extract standardized to 0.8–1 percent taken 30–60 minutes before bedtime. Valerian has been noted to lead to excessive drowsiness in some people who take it along with other antidepressant or anti-anxiety medications, so again, talk with your doctor if you are considering valerian to make sure it does not have negative interactions with medications (prescribed or over-the-counter) you might already be taking.

Lavender is an essential oil that smells pleasing to almost everyone. Though it isn't a hypnotic itself, it does help to set the stage for sleep by calming and soothing the nervous system. It is available in multiple forms, including an essential-oil-filled capsule under a trade name. Consider buying an eye mask weighted with lavender-scented beads, applying the essential oil topically, diffusing it into your room, adding it to your nightly bath, or using ingestible essential oil in your tea at night. Be mindful of drinking too much liquid before bed, as this may increase nighttime urination, which could interfere with sleep.

Traditional Pharmaceuticals Often Used for Sleep. Some over-the-counter and prescribed pharmaceuticals are directly marketed for sleep therapy, and others are used "off label" (meaning they're not FDA approved for sleep per se but are used mostly because of their helpful side effects).

First let's talk about antihistamines, which includes over-the-counter medications like diphenhydramine (brand name Benadryl) and doxylamine (Unisom) and prescription medications like hydroxyzine (Vistaril) and doxepin (Silenor). Many people with insomnia have tried antihistamines, but they are typically not recommended for a number of reasons, most notably their potential side effects of dizziness, low blood pressure, and lightheadedness when changing positions. This can be especially dangerous in patients who are elderly or at increased risk of falls. These same effects (anticholinergic effects) can suppress our REM sleep, leading to less restorative sleep even when they work. Due to their relatively long half-life (the rate at which the medication is eliminated from the body), they can also leave patients with a "hangover" in the morning, a feeling of lethargy that can make mornings difficult. Additionally, antihistamines lose their effectiveness with more than 2 weeks of continued use, which can lead to psychological addiction, in which patients are convinced they help with sleep even though the actual effect is minimal. Finally, research has pointed to memory issues related to antihistamine use (Gray et al., 2015).

Next on our list are traditional hypnotic pharmaceuticals. This is what most doctors think of when asked by patients to prescribe something for sleep. One group is non-benzodiazepine hypnotics, which includes zolpidem (Ambien), zaleplon (Sonata), and eszopiclone (Lunesta). These drugs strengthen the brain's response to the relaxation neurotransmitter GABA (gamma-aminobutyric acid), which essentially slows brain activity, making us feel drowsy. Medicines in this class take about 30 minutes to work and last about 8 hours, so it's important to take only when you can allot a full night's rest. There's also a dissolvable low-dose zolpidem

(Intermezzo) with a shorter half-life, meaning that it is eliminated from the body more quickly, so it can be taken in the middle of the night. Other types of hypnotics that are currently less commonly known include the orexin receptor agonist suvorexant (Belsomra) and melatonin receptor agonist ramelteon (Rozerem).

Patients frequently state that they are taking one of these medications for insomnia but often still take hours to fall asleep. If that's the case, the medication is likely not working well, and you should consider another type of treatment (have a discussion with your doctor).

All of the hypnotics are developed for short-term use, not years and years on end as many people take them. Hypnotics can have disturbing side effects, including memory problems, sleep walking, and vivid dreaming, not to mention impaired mental alertness the next day. Additionally, a physical tolerance may build up with prolonged use, meaning that the same amount of medication may not produce the same effect once taken for a while. In addition to a physical dependence, a psychological dependence frequently develops, too—you may think you need it to sleep when, in fact, it is really not doing all that much.

Note: It is best to avoid alcohol when using hypnotics since they act on the same GABA receptors, relaxing your muscles too much, and may stop your breathing in the middle of the night.

All of this being said, hypnotics are an option for many people with insomnia, but they shouldn't be the *only* intervention. As we hope you've learned already in this book, other treatment strategies do exist, and it is best to try nonpharmacological interventions first, followed by herbal strategies. The quick fix isn't always the best method for long-term health.

Acupuncture. Acupuncture is one of my favorite tools to address my patient's problems. Acupuncture is a method in the ancient system of traditional Chinese medicine (TCM) where tiny disposable needles are inserted into the body at specific points along established energy meridians to balance the vital life force, called Qi (pronounced "chee"). In

TCM, problems in the body happen when chi is out of balance, some-times described using words like "excessive" or "deficient" or "stagnant" chi. Insomnia can be due to any of these descriptions, so TCM practi-tioners use patterns of symptoms to ascertain what acupuncture points to use. The World Health Organization publishes a list of medical con-ditions for which acupuncture is approved based on available medical science, and insomnia is one of these approved conditions. Finding a licensed acupuncturist (with an "LAc" certification) or a medical doctor who provides acupuncture is, fortunately, becoming relatively easy.

Co-occurring Stress and Anxiety

I think about stress and anxiety as being on a continuum. It's tough to know exactly when feeling stressed starts to feel like anxiety. When stress persists for an extended period of time, our bodies and minds are not able to cope. Insomnia often happens alongside anxiety (and with depression, as I discuss later) and requires its own focused treatment. One of the first signs of anxiety and depression can be a change in sleep pattern. Restful sleep contributes significantly to our mental health, so poor sleep can make anxiety and depression symptoms feel even worse. When we begin to lose sleep and start to worry about our performance, we perpetuate the cycle of sleeplessness and anxiety.

The three basic categories to approach stress and anxiety that affect your sleep are the same as for simple insomnia—herbs and supplements, pharmaceuticals, and TCM—but the choices are typically different.

Herbs and Supplements. Botanicals to address anxiety are everywhere. The following are my favorites to use in clinical practice; this is not meant to be an exhaustive list. The class of herbs to treat mood disorders and stress are called *adaptogens*, meaning they help us adapt to external conditions more effectively. Seems fitting, right?

My favorite adaptogen is lemon balm. I keep lemon balm in my own medicine cabinet at all times. As most herbs do, lemon balm works on a number of receptors in the body. Its primary mechanism of action is relaxation through the GABA receptors in our brain. A cousin of mint, lemon balm is a gentle suggestion to the mind and body to relax. To me, lemon balm feels like I've had half a glass of wine. It has additional mechanisms in the body, including an effect on the gastrointestinal tract, which can make it beneficial for those who suffer from irritable bowel syndrome in addition to anxiety. It can be taken any time of day and dosed as needed, so it could be used just before an anxiety-provoking situation like a big presentation at work or just before airplane takeoff. One summer, I grew lemon balm in a pot on my porch and used the leaves to make a tea with a French coffee press. It was medicinally, minty tasting, and boy was it relaxing—what a treat! The most common ways to find lemon balm are in tea, as a tincture (where an herb's essence is suspended in a small amount of alcohol), or in capsule form either alone or with other herbs. If you buy a tincture form, you can take it straight or add it to hot water and lemon to make your own tea.

Another useful supplement to help with anxiety is L-theanine. This is an amino acid and naturally occurs in protein sources and tea. L-theanine promotes relaxation without necessarily making us sleepy, so it's very useful when we are "tired but wired" so that once our mind is turned off we have no problem falling asleep. Like lemon balm, its mechanism of action is mostly on GABA receptors, but it has other mechanisms as well. It can also be used during the day when feeling anxious. Typical dosing is 100 mg twice daily or 200 mg at night about 30 minutes before bed.

An unsung hero in the management of stress and anxiety in chamomile. Chamomile tea is a staple in my kitchen, and I often travel with a few tea bags. In addition to easing the mind, chamomile eases the gut and aids in digestion, making it a perfect 8 p.m. drink (but remember to limit liquids within 3 hours of going to bed!). I often encourage my patients to reestablish a bedtime routine since our bodies like predictable rhythms, and chamomile tea is an excellent start to your evening ritual. My recommendation is two bags of chamomile tea steeped in 4–8 ounces of hot water for 10 minutes. Consider letting it steep while you take your bath, and then drink it while snuggling in your favorite chair with a book. If your nighttime bladder is sensitive, you may do better with a chamomile tincture (the volume is significant less than tea) or omitting the chamomile altogether.

Traditional Pharmaceutical Options. Pharmaceutical medications to address anxiety are often used "off-label" to induce sleepiness with the added benefit of helping an associated mood disorder. The best example of this is the use of benzodiazepines for anxiety-related sleep issues. Benzodiazepines include medications like clonazepam (Klonopin), diazepam (Valium), lorazepam (Ativan), and alprazolam (Xanax), among others. Each medication has a different half-life (the rate at which a medication is eliminated from the body), which helps a health care practitioner decide which medication is most likely to be helpful for your particular situation. Benzodiazepines act on benzodiazepine-specific receptors, which enhance the relaxation neurotransmitter GABA.

Benzodiazepines are meant to be used short term for confined situations. It's common in practice to see patients with a small prescription for, say, Ativan, to use when flying or during an MRI, if those are anxiety-provoking situations. In sleep medicine, if patients have an acute change in sleep habits as a result of a temporary stressor like the recent death of a loved one, benzodiazepines may be helpful, but this requires a discussion of the benefits and risks with their doctor.

Benzodiazepines sound like a miracle drug for anxiety, right? Well, not exactly. It's easy to become both physically and emotionally addicted to these substances. We build physical tolerance to benzodiazepines, so increasing amounts of medication are needed to achieve the same effect over time. The emotional vacation that can take place with use of benzodiazepines makes them a danger for psychological addiction, so they are not practical on an ongoing basis.

For many, a better pharmaceutical treatment for anxiety in the longer term is an selective serotonin reuptake inhibitor (SSRI). This class of medication engages the feel-good hormone serotonin, which indirectly helps with sleep. Typical SSRIs include sertraline (Zoloft), fluoxetine (Prozac), paroxetine (Paxil), citalopram (Celexa), and escitalopram (Lexapro). Pharmaceutical cousins of SSRIs include medications like venlafaxine (Effexor), mirtazapine (Remeron), and bupropion (Wellbutrin), which include effects on other neurotransmitters like norepinephrine or dopamine or effects on the sympathetic (fight-or-flight) nervous system. The dosing of SSRIs and their counterparts determines whether they have anti-anxiety or antidepressant effects. Some SSRIs are better for anxiety, and some are better for depression. A good primary doctor or psychiatrist can lead you in the right direction.

Similar to SSRIs are the pharmaceutical class of tricyclic antidepressants (TCAs), a much older class of medications that include amitriptyline (Elavil), nortriptyline (Pamelor), and doxepin (Silenor). These days most TCAs are used off-label to treat other conditions, as they are no longer first-line treatment for mood disorders. One common complaint of TCA users is drowsiness, which is why they are often used to treat concurrent sleep issues.

Traditional Chinese Medicine. TCM and acupuncture can be a valuable asset in the treatment of sleep disorders that have an anxiety or stress component. Acupuncture has a beautiful way of settling the mind during a treatment. I personally feel this sensation as heaviness, or grounding, that seems to anchor my body to the table. When we are anxious or worried, our Qi, our vital life energy, can feel all over the place. It's as if the frazzled nature of our minds spreads into our whole being. By working on the meridians that govern this anxious energy, acupuncture can help to settle the mind.

Co-occurring Depression

Depression can often manifest in our sleep patterns. Typically we see issues with early morning awakening at 3 or 4 a.m. with difficulty reinitiating sleep, but not everyone is a textbook case. Depression can also mimic some anxiety symptoms, but with a subtle difference. While the underlying emotion in anxiety is worry, the basement emotion in depression is sadness or a lack of interest in things you usually enjoy.

Supplements. Just like with stress and anxiety, a number of herbs and supplements are useful in the management of depression. One of my favorites based on my clinical practice is SAMe (S-adenosylmethionine), and while scientific data suggests it is helpful, the data are not conclusive. SAMe is a molecule formed naturally in the body that supports production of our feel-good hormones. SAMe can also be helpful for patients who struggle with both chronic pain issues and depression, as often found in disorders like fibromyalgia. Since SAMe lifts the mood, caution is advised in those with bipolar disorder or anxious states, as it could precipitate more anxiety. In general, best dosing strategies are to start slow, so I recommend 200 mg twice daily for a few days and then increasing by 200 mg every few days up to a maximum dose of 600 mg twice daily. It's also important to make sure you have good B vitamin intake while on SAMe, which helps its breakdown in the body.

Another useful supplement in the treatment of depression is 5-HTP (5-hydroxytrytophan). 5-HTP is a naturally occurring amino acid involved in the production of serotonin, one of our feel-good neurotransmitters. Typical doses of 5-HTP are 100–300 mg per day in divided doses, but it's moderately sedating, so sleep dosing is 50–100 mg about 30 minutes before bedtime.

Pharmaceuticals. Similar to the treatment of anxiety, we can use SSRIs to treat depression. The reason we can use the same medication to treat both anxiety and depression is that the dosing and individual drug pharmacology determine whether it has an antidepressant or an anti-anxiety effect. As a class, SSRIs increase the power of the feel-good hormone serotonin, which occasionally benefits sleep as well.

Although less common, some physicians still like to use TCAs as a treatment for depression. As discussed above regarding stress and anxiety, TCAs are no longer first-line treatments for depression, but they can be useful in patients who do not respond to first-line drugs. They also tend to make patients sleepy, hence their use in patients with insomnia.

Traditional Chinese Medicine. In TCM depression is considered literally "stuck" or stagnant energy that weighs us down. TCM describes all of life as a balance—most of us are familiar with the balance of yin and yang. While yin is cooling, nourishing, and calming, yang is heating and energetic. We need an equilibrium of yin and yang to function well. When there's too much yin because of a relative yang deficiency, depression can present. TCM practitioners teach that the best way to get out of that stuck feeling is to move your Qi, with both exercise and acupuncture.

Co-occurring Chronic Pain

Proper treatment of pain can certainly influence sleep for the better. When we have acute pain that lasts a few days to a few weeks, it generally doesn't have a long-lasting effect on our sleep. Chronic pain, however, is a different animal. We know from extensive chronic pain research that it's not just an external stimulus that lead to a pain; it's a complex disorder changing the brain's pain signals in a way that affects every part of our lives, including our sleep.

Addressing insomnia due to chronic pain starts with getting comfortable in bed. If you haven't invested in a supportive mattress, high-quality linens, or a great pillow, now is your time—doctor's orders!

Positioning in bed is everything. Have a few pillows available to make yourself comfortable. Try one under your knees if you lie on your back. Try a body pillow to hug if you sleep on your side. Also give care to the pillow you place your head on. One of my favorite pillows for chronic neck pain is one that's filled with water. It's heavy and not movable during sleep and dynamically molds to the head and neck.

Herbs and Supplements. Some botanicals and supplements are helpful for managing pain. For *myofascial pain*, defined as pain in our muscles and surrounding connective tissue called fascia, one of my favorite supplements is magnesium, discussed earlier in this chapter. Magnesium is helpful for myofascial pain, the most common reason for low back and neck pain. Typical dosing is 400 mg at night.

For pain associated with osteoarthritis, a great supplement is a combination of ginger and turmeric. At our practice at the Stamford Health Center for Integrative Medicine and Wellness, ginger and turmeric is one of our most commonly recommended botanical combinations. Ginger and turmeric have a multitude of mechanisms, but the most important one here is COX-2 inhibition, similar to NSAIDs (nonsteroidal anti-inflammatory drugs) like meloxicam (Mobic), naproxen (Aleve), and ibuprofen (Advil) but with less risk to the kidneys and stomach. For turmeric to be effective outside the gastrointestinal system, it needs to be taken with piperine, or black pepper alkaloids. Typical dosing is 500 mg of each, twice daily.

For neuropathic pain and chronic pruritis (itching), a useful supplement is evening primrose oil. This oil is rich in gamma-linolenic acid, an omega-6 fatty acid that, unlike other omega 6 fatty acids, is very anti-inflammatory and has a nerve-modulating effect, making it especially useful for peripheral neuropathy and chronic pruritis. Typical dosing is 1300 mg twice daily.

Another bothersome condition that prevents restful sleep is restless legs syndrome (RLS). RLS presents as an uncomfortable feeling of needing to move the legs while in a resting position. Sometimes this manifests as an internal restlessness, and sometimes as a creepy-crawly feeling on the legs. One association between nutrition and RLS is adequate intake of iron. Many women tend to be deficient in iron because of the menstrual period, as the body requires iron to make more red blood cells after the loss of blood each month; however, both men and women can be mildly insufficient in iron due to poor dietary habits. True iron deficiency leads to anemia, but checking your serum ferritin level can be helpful if you suspect you are iron insufficient. Serum ferritin should be over 100 ng/ml, but it's often not flagged because the reference range of most labs can be from 9 to 300 ng/ml. When it comes to vitamins and minerals, most integrative practitioners like to see their patients closer to the middle of the reference range.

Pharmaceuticals. Numerous pharmaceuticals are on the market to help with pain, but a few stand out due to their positive impact on sleep. Let's start with gabapentin (Neurontin). Gabapentin has long been known to help with neuropathic pain, which is pain resulting from irritation and inflammation of nerve fibers. How gabapentin works isn't completely understood, but it dampens pain signals by affecting calcium channels. Dosages depend on the severity of the condition but can extend to 1200 mg three times a day if needed. The most common complaint of gabapentin is sleepiness, which makes it a great medication for helping with insomnia as a result of pain conditions, but this can limit its dosing during daytime hours. Patients may also complain of dizziness, so caution is advised in elderly patients who may be at risk for falls. It is usually best to start low and slow with this medication and work with your doctor to gradually increase to a dose that reduces your pain.

A newer drug on the market to help with pain and its related conditions is pregabalin (Lyrica). Pregabalin works similarly to gabapentin, and like gabapentin, common side effects include drowsiness and dizziness. Pregabalin is probably best known to help with fibromyalgia and neuropathic pain conditions ranging from postherpetic neuralgia to diabetic nerve pain. Doses range widely, depending on the condition being treated, with a maximum dose of 600 mg per day.

Traditional Chinese Medicine. TCM views pain as an energy imbalance. Sometimes there's a blockage of Qi, and when Qi gets stuck and stagnant it can manifest as pain. Other times there's a deficient amount of Qi moving in the body. Qi is supported by proper nutrition and good circulation, so deficient energy is believed to result from an imbalance in these factors. Acupuncture can be provided along TCM meridians, or can be done at the areas of tenderness, called Ashi points. It's generally understood that acupuncture can stimulate production of endorphins and regulate neurotransmitters, which can reduce electrical activity in the area of the brain involved in pain perception. I recommend trying four to six acupuncture visits each about 1 week apart to see if it's helpful.

Trigger point therapy is related to acupuncture. I usually describe it to patients as a Western kind of Ashi acupuncture. In short, myofascial trigger points are areas in the fascia surrounding our skeletal muscles that are extremely sensitive to touch and generally radiate outside the exact location being stimulated. Subjectively, we feel trigger points as the "knot" or muscle spasm from which more widespread pain arises. Imagine a massage therapist massaging your shoulders and then he finds what I call the "money spot"—the spot that hurts so good. That's a trigger point. The reason we feel this discomfort spread outside the exact place he's touching is due to fascial planes. Imagine that all of your muscles are covered with plastic wrap. That's the fascia. All the plastic wrap on all of your muscles "talks" to adjacent plastic wrap, and those signals can travel throughout the body. This idea explains why stimulating a trigger point in the neck can often lead to a strange feeling in the jaw, in the chest, or down the arm.

Putting a needle in a trigger point helps release the muscle spasm that exists in the tight band of muscle fibers. Often the muscle will feel a bit worse for a few hours, and then it will feel better. This improvement in pain could last anywhere from a few hours to a few days or even longer. Since myofascial pain is the most common reason for neck and back pain, this therapy can provide significant relief to patients and allow for more restorative sleep.

Perimenopause

I once heard a doctor say, "Perimenopause is the best seven to ten years of your life!" I repeat that phrase to my patients often, since many women are not prepared for how long their symptoms will last.

Our menstrual cycles should be fairly regular throughout our reproductive lifetime. Generally, most women experience a relatively predictable monthly ovulation when our ovary releases an egg, followed by a menstrual period 14 days later. During our middle forties we transition from mostly ovulatory cycles to more *anovulatory* cycles (meaning that the ovary doesn't release an egg), which lead to irregular bleeding patterns—this is the start of *perimenopause*. Those irregular bleeding patterns continue until the period is farther and farther apart. Once we go one full year without a menstrual period, that particular date is defined as the onset of *menopause*. Thereafter, we are considered postmenopausal.

The fluctuations in our sex hormones like estrogen and progesterone during perimenopause can bring about a whole host of symptoms. In addition to light or heavy periods, with varying breast tenderness, uterine cramping, vaginal dryness, irritability, and fatigue, we can also start to have hot flashes and night sweats. Night sweats can vary from waking up feeling warm to full-on soaks that drench your pajamas and bed sheets. Whatever the intensity of the night sweat, as most women know, any interruption to sleep is not good. Many women report significant difficulty getting back to sleep, especially when the night sweat occurs in the early morning hours. This leads to further fatigue and irritability.

Thankfully, there are a number of solutions to manage perimenopausal symptoms. As many of you know, the gold standard is hormone therapy with estrogen and progesterone, but it is possible to manage symptoms without hormones.

Herbs and Supplements. Many botanicals exist on the market, so many that I cannot discuss them all here. But here are the herbs I recommend most often.

The backbone herb of perimenopausal management is black cohosh. This herb falls into the adaptogen category—it helps us adapt to changing circumstances. It works by occupying estrogen receptors, which not only helps with vasomotor symptoms like hot flashes and night sweats but also it helps with irritability. I typically recommend approximately 40 mg twice daily. Additionally, many products come in both daytime and nighttime formulations, with the nighttime supplements including other herbs for sleep.

Another useful supplement during perimenopause is evening primrose oil. As mentioned above, evening primrose oil is rich in the anti-inflammatory omega 6 fatty acid gamma-linolenic acid. Evening primrose oil helps modulate the nervous system, which helps decrease the unpleasantness of hot flashes and night sweats. Additionally, evening primrose oil has been studied as an aid for breast pain, another common complaint of perimenopause. Dosing is 1300 mg twice daily.

Pharmaceuticals. Gabapentin (Neurontin) is often used off-label to manage vasomotor symptoms like hot flashes, and it's very effective for many women. One downside is that gabapentin must be dosed three times per day, but that's also an upside because it allows for dosing only when it's needed, and you can alter your doses throughout the day depending on how bothersome your symptoms are. Since gabapentin is mildly sedating, most of my patients either omit it or take smaller doses during the day and then a slightly larger dose at night. Additionally, it takes a very small amount of medication to work, usually 100–300 mg three times per day.

SSRIs like paroxetine (Paxil) and escitalopram (Lexapro) are being specifically marketed to women for the management of hot flashes, but physicians have been using other drugs in that class for years. A cousin to SSRIs, venlafaxine (Effexor) works on dopamine and norepinephrine in addition to serotonin. It can also be helpful to manage irritability and vasomotor symptoms. Typical dosages of venlafaxine are 37.5 mg twice daily or 75 mg extended release once daily, but doses can be higher if symptoms warrant.

And of course, there's hormone therapy with estrogen and progesterone, the gold standard in management of symptoms for many years. After all, what we are missing during perimenopause is the predictable release of these hormones! Hormone therapy delivers a steady state of estrogen and progesterone (or just estrogen if a women has had a hysterectomy), but it has now fallen out of favor as a universal recommendation due to findings of the Women's Health Initiative (WHI). The WHI was an extensive research program started in the 1990s to understand common causes of death and disability in postmenopausal women. One of the major findings of the WHI was that hormone therapy increased the risk of breast cancer and stroke (Rossouw et al., 2002). If you choose to use hormones, most gynecologists cap use at 5–7 years, but there are certainly exceptions, and a discussion with your doctor about the risks and benefits is warranted. If you haven't responded to any other standard behavioral or pharmacological treatments for sleep and you are finding it more and more difficult to get through the day due to increasing fatigue, some form of hormone therapy might be indicated based on your personal history.

When prescribing hormones, many gynecologists opt for traditional birth control pills to provide hormone relief at the beginning of perimenopause. At the end of perimenopause or when postmenopausal, women use hormone therapy in patch, topical cream, or oral forms.

"Bioidentical hormone therapy" simply means that the hormones being prescribed are identical to the forms naturally found in the body.

There are pharmaceutical formulations like Estrace that are bioidentical, but they come only in certain doses. Some providers and patients prefer a more individual approach and use compounded hormones. *Compounded medications* are specially made for an individual patient at whatever dose the doctor decides and come in a variety of forms, including topical, oral, sublingual (under the tongue), vaginal, rectal, or buccal (absorbed in between the cheek and teeth). Compounding is usually more expensive than traditional pharmaceuticals.

Traditional Chinese Medicine. TCM has a unique view on the perimeno-pausal transition. It describes this transition as energy rising in the body, as we move from being mothers of the womb to becoming mothers of our hearts—beautiful, right? As this energy rises it brings about the energetic changes of hot flashes and night sweats, mood changes, and difficulty sleeping. TCM also describes perimenopause as an imbalance in yin and yang caused by a deficiency in yin. Our yin, which is cooling and nour-ishing to the body, is supported by estrogen. As our estrogen wanes with menopause, we lose that anchoring balance. What remains is unbal-anced yang, which is hot and unyielding—the prototypical hot flash put into words. Using modalities like acupuncture, TCM understands peri-menopausal treatment to be a rebalancing of yin and yang by building the waning yin, thus bringing harmony to our bodies.

CONCLUSION

- Proper lifestyle interventions starting with diet, exercise, and stress management, which, along with restorative sleep, create the fertile ground in which we can plant the seeds of CBT-I, herbal and pharmaceutical medications, and acupuncture.
- Seek out an integrative practitioner near you to coach you on your quest to better health.

15.

What to Do When Life Gets
in the Way of Sleep

ull disclosure: I waited until the end of writing this book to start this chapter. Why? Because, while I am a sleep doctor and clinical psychologist who prioritizes sleep and well-being, I also know that no one is perfect . . . especially me. There isn't always a simple magic solution to that loudly snoring husband who is in complete denial that he's impacting your sleep, or magic fairies that will miraculously come and make lunches every night for the kids while we catch up on other chores from the day. I'm well aware that it is a juggling act—we women are prone to taking on far too much from time to time. And sometimes—more than I'd like to admit—I drop all the balls on the floor, big time.

At least once or twice a week, a patient or friend asks me, "How do you sleep?" (or "How do your kids sleep?")—almost as if to test how I'm doing and if I follow my own rules. I think most people are surprised when I'm honest with them. Some nights aren't great, either due to my own issues getting in the way (such as writing way too late into the night, when I know I should have stopped an hour earlier but lost track of the time), my daughter calling out for me after a nightmare, or my husband getting up really early to go to a meeting in the city and accidentally waking me up. These things all happen, and while I have times when I either have bouts of insomnia (when I just can't sleep because my mind won't turn off even though I really want to) or simply don't make sleep a priority, I've learned to brush off a bad night or two and work to make things consistent, to line up as best as possible in my life, so that a good night's sleep is one of the top things on my list to work toward.

Some people might joke with me about being such a lover of sleep, but I know that if we make sleep a priority, it will in turn make the rest of our lives just that much easier. Good sleep helps the rest of my life fall into place just a little bit better. I find it ironic that some parents place so much emphasis on their kid's sleep schedule, to the point of rigidity with bedtimes, wake times, and naps, but when the time comes for them to keep a consistent schedule themselves, all rules are out the window. If you keep a good routine with your own sleep, unwind at the end of the day to set the stage for sleep, and really are consistent *most* nights, you reap the benefits and lessen your risk of developing or worsening insomnia. Making sleep a priority and getting the proper treatment for any sleep problems you might have will only work in your favor throughout life.

I'm well aware of how often I've said throughout this book that, for women with insomnia, a huge problem is trying to force oneself to sleep at night and placing too much emphasis on being able to sleep. While that's definitely an issue, I also see lots of women who are burning the candle at both ends. They don't make relaxation and winding down a priority and, as a result, struggle with falling asleep because the sleep stage wasn't set properly—remember, sleep isn't an on/off switch; we need to treat it like a dimmer switch. And when they do finally decide to unwind and relax, they often get so caught up in binge-watching TV that they lose track of all time, perpetuating an endless cycle of forced sleep deprivation and insomnia. I've also clinically noticed over the years that women come to me desperate to get some sleep because their brains are racing all day and night. However, once their insomnia is under control, getting them to keep a more regular sleep/wake schedule and be consistent with the sleep guidelines in this book becomes a challenge because "there's just too much to do and I can't make time for sleep." Sleep, once such a precious commodity, is now forgotten in the pile of laundry by the stairs.

THE CASE OF THE SNORING BED PARTNER

I think I can count on two hands the number of patients I've worked with in my career where both the patient and the bed partner have had insomnia. I think I hear, on a daily basis, "My husband can fall asleep at the drop of a hat and sleeps like a log." Then they add, "a loud, snoring log." This topic was touched on in Chapter 8: it is important to have a discussion with your bed partner about any snoring, choking, or gasping during sleep or body movements, jerking, or thrashing in the middle of the night that might be impacting your own sleep. If you're concerned it is a problem, speak up. If your bed partner denies the issue altogether, try to take a stance of concern for your partner's health and overall sleep quality, as opposed to using an accusatory tone.

Believe it or not, I've had patients record their bed partners (only with permission!) at night to show them the issue at hand. If the bed partner then refuses to get treatment or won't follow treatment recommendations, and the noise or nighttime movements are simply too disruptive to your own sleep at night, larger issues in the relationship likely need to be addressed. An open discussion about respect of your own health, safety, and sleep quality is paramount. And the person with untreated sleep apnea is often quite sleepy and may be at risk of dozing while driving due to excessive daytime sleepiness.

If this still doesn't help or there is nothing that can be done just yet to effectively manage the snoring or nighttime movements, it might just be easiest to make a conscious decision to sleep in different beds or different rooms. Sleeping separately can be extremely freeing for some couples. They get in bed at the beginning of the night to snuggle and have sex if desired, but once bedtime comes around, they retreat to separate beds/bedrooms to sleep. The improved sleep quality leads to less resentment toward each other in the end. However, as I said, it really needs to be a discussion and decision made together; otherwise, hurt feelings are likely to happen.

BABIES AND YOUNG CHILDREN

Realistic expectations must to be set regarding what is considered normal versus abnormal sleep for the first few months of having a new baby in the house. Structure is nonexistent in a newborn's sleep schedule since a circadian rhythm has not yet been established. New parents need to expect that sleep will be disrupted by frequent nighttime feedings for the first 3 months or so of the baby's life and that this is par for the course with a newborn. Young babies sleep a good deal; the issue for parents is that it is in such short chunks (2–3 hours at a time) that we can't get a long stretch of sleep ourselves.

Realize as well that you're not a supermom. Even though we want to do everything alone without much (or any) help, get assistance wherever and whenever you can. Create a game plan with your spouse regarding feedings, diaper changes, laundry, and so on. If you're bottle feeding, split up the night so you take half the feedings and your partner does the other half. If you're solely breastfeeding, consider asking your partner to take care of diapers or bring the baby to you or put the baby back in the crib—these are all things that can help balance out the workload and allow for slightly more sleep during the rollercoaster with a newborn. If you have the finances to do so, even consider getting a night nurse at the beginning, even for a night or two every week. The nurse can help you learn strategies to get your baby to sleep better and take some of the burden from you at night (even if you are breastfeeding). Finally, a lot of the time women are told to "sleep when the baby sleeps." While short naps are definitely helpful for most moms, it can be difficult to turn the brain off when you're always keeping an ear and eye out for a newborn that could wake up at any time. Make sure to rest during this time and get in some relaxation whenever possible. Plus, keep in mind that if your baby is sleeping longer stretches at night but still napping during the day (as babies should do for a few years!), you might not want to nap alongside your baby if it is impacting your own nighttime sleep.

While a detailed discussion of pediatric sleep medicine is beyond the scope of this book, it is important to recognize how young children's sleep (or lack thereof) greatly influences the mother's slumber. On occasion, I see women in my practice who complain of returning to sleep in the middle of the night and awakening earlier than desired. After some discussion, it becomes clear that most of the times the awakening is due to a child in the house either calling out for mom or coming into the bedroom in the middle of the night. Mom then does whatever she can to get her child back to sleep but is now usually wide awake from the child coming in, or sometimes has a wriggly young preschooler in the bed or even sleeping on the floor next to the crib. Sound familiar? What needs to be done here, first and foremost, is to get the child on a better behavioral sleep plan. Many fantastic resources are available for pediatric behavioral sleep medicine; I list some of my favorites in the Appendix of Resources at the back of the book.

I won't go into a lengthy talk here about what you can do, since each child's and family's circumstances and needs are different, but there are some things that should be in place at the outset to help give structure to your child's sleep, thereby allowing predictability for your own sleep pattern. Sleep deprivation, late bedtimes/early awakenings, skipping naps (most kids still need a nap up until age 3, and some continue napping until age 5!), and poor sleep hygiene all wreak havoc on a young child's sleep. Make sure your child is in bed, getting the recommended amount of sleep per night. (For great, sleep-specialist-approved information, see the Pediatric Sleep Council's website at www.babysleep.com.)

Babies and children thrive on routine, and giving structure to their sleep and nap schedule helps prevent an overtired child. Often we think that a later bedtime might help with a faster time to fall asleep when in fact the exact opposite is true. A tired child doesn't usually look sleepy; instead, the child will be irritable and cranky and become hyper, making sleep a tough thing to settle down into. Earlier bedtimes, regular naps whenever possible, and consistency are key here.

We've grown so accustomed to having electronics and monitors tell us everything at all times that we don't rely as much on our own gut and common sense. Baby monitors can easily disrupt a mom's sleep with static and small normal noises that the baby makes in the middle of the night. Plus, some have a light or screen on them that cannot easily be dimmed, further lighting up the room. If the baby is nearby where you could easily hear any cries, consider turning the monitor off at night while you're asleep and turning it on only when you are concerned. This way, every tiny noise and piece of light won't wake you up. Or, if that's hard to tolerate (or baby is farther away in the house), turn the monitor volume down much lower or even move it across the room so you can get some better sleep.

I'm also often asked about putting a baby to bed later so that the parents can spend time with their child after a busy workday. This inherently isn't an issue, as long as the child is kept on a consistent sleep/wake schedule daily and allowed to sleep a full night with the appropriate recommended hours of sleep on a regular basis. Essentially, a later bedtime nightly is fine, but only if a later wake time is allowed every morning, too. Otherwise, you will have to deal with a sleep-deprived child, one who might be overtired come bedtime and risk not sleeping as well at night. Keep in mind, this might become a problem when the child is older and has to go to preschool!

TECH, TEENAGERS, AND THE NIGHT OWLS THEY BECOME

As our little children grow into adolescence, their sleep and social schedules frequently impact mom's sleep. Young children who are good sleepers typically go to bed early and rise early, but as they hit the early teenage years, there is a natural delay in the circadian rhythm to go to bed later and wake up later (hence the push for later school start times in middle and high school). Struggles between parents and teens frequently occur during weeknights when the parents want the child to be in bed earlier to get enough sleep for school. Big frustrations often arise on weekends and summer vacations when high school and college students go out late with friends, only to return home late with mom waiting up for her child to arrive safely.

While a healthy balance between an ideal sleep/wake pattern and what might be appropriate for a teenager on summer breaks is quite difficult for many people to reach, make sure you set limits with your teen and practice what you preach. Electronics (especially phones, tablets, and computers) are huge contributors to delayed sleep patterns in adolescents, and setting up a family electronic charging station in a kitchen or common area might be of use to keep all electronics out of everyone's bedroom. If you tell your teenager not to have a phone in bed, you need to do your best to do the exact same thing, as it will only improve your sleep as well and will set a good example. There are apps you can download and timers you can set to turn off the Wi-Fi at predetermined times, further reducing temptation for teens to use social media and texting while at home. For weekends and summer nights out, distress tolerance is tough for many parents, but accepting that you've taught your child to be responsible and done all you can to ensure his or her safety , while also accepting that we cannot keep our children safe and 100 percent protected at all times, is key. Set a reasonable curfew and stick to it. Being consistent with limits and rules is crucial here.

If you can, try to go to sleep at your usual bedtime even if your teen isn't home. However, if you do wake up once your child walks in the door to alert you your child is home (or if you never fell asleep to begin with!), just accept that you might be startled or have trouble getting to sleep right away and know that this teenager phase, too, shall pass. Consider sharing the "night watch" responsibilities with a significant other if possible—Friday night you stay up in the den, and Saturday night your partner does.

CARING FOR AGING PARENTS

It is a tough situation for many people who take on the role of caretaker for elderly parents. It is not as easy to shape the behavior of some older adults with dementia to sleep through the night, though making sure you keep the room dark (use night-lights) but safe at night (guard rails, gates at the top of the stairs) and as bright as possible during the day can help consolidate nighttime sleep. It can be tough to get a good night's sleep when you're being called for multiple times at night or worried that a parent might wander off. Try to take as many precautions as possible, problem solve in advance, and encourage the older adult to keep proper sleep hygiene and a consistent sleep/wake schedule. Discuss your concerns with your parent's doctors. This is another instance where help is a necessity in many circumstances. Is a night nurse or home health aid possible? And if you have a rough night, as mentioned earlier in this book, it is important to practice acceptance that there is not much you can do that night.

ME TIME: CHOOSING NETFLIX OVER SLEEP

It feels so nice to have quiet time at night—everyone is asleep in bed and you finally have some peace and quiet. Instead of going to sleep as well or winding down without screens, many women choose to lie on the couch and catch up on TV. This is "my time" to relax. Yes, it feels great in the moment, but we need to be mindful of just how much screen-time relaxing we do, as it can impact our body's ability to fall asleep and stay asleep once we make the decision to actually go to bed. Recall the familiar story of many women falling asleep on the couch while watching TV, only to later move to the bed, further reinforcing a vicious cycle of insomnia.

I love a good TV show, and I have some reality show pleasures as well that I find hard to turn off without seeing who wins the series (hands up high for the *Great British Baking Show*!). With the plethora of streaming TV at our fingertips, it can often feel as if there's too much content to keep up with and we'll never consume it all. Research is starting to come out regarding the phenomenon of binge-watching. There's a certain social element to it, bringing people together to discuss and experience storylines from start to finish in a quick and easy way, on their own timeline, and on whatever device they want. Here's the problem, though: we are choosing immediate gratification over sleep, and at a time when sound decision making isn't as easy to do. Recall what I said above: often people with insomnia want to sleep but can't, but then when their insomnia is actually much better they don't make the time for sleep. Cue binge-watching. A study published in the *Journal of Clinical Sleep Medicine* suggested that women binge-watch TV more than men and that one in ten people binge-watch TV on a weekly basis (Exelmans & Van den Bulck, 2017). Results showed that poorer sleep quality, insomnia, and fatigue were associated with greater levels of binge-watching, likely fueled by an overactive brain from watching TV.

Not only is getting caught up in binge-watching for prolonged time an issue with restricting your bedtime, but the excessive blue light exposure limits melatonin production, making it harder to wind down and fall asleep (as discussed throughout this book). As a result, it becomes harder to turn off your brain and go to bed. When catching up with TV at night, make sure to set some limits for yourself in order to make sleep a priority as well. Set an episode limit nightly *before* you start watching your series, for example, "Tonight I'll watch two episodes of *Arrested Development*."

Make sure to wear blue-blocking glasses at night or use blue-blocking apps for tablets and computers to help combat melatonin-suppressing blue light. Stop and take a 5-minute breather and stretch break between each episode. Don't just let it go right into the next episode without mindfully taking a break, or episodes will link together faster than you can appreciate. Find time on the weekend to catch up on your shows—nighttime midweek shouldn't be the only time to zone out. Make sure to watch these shows outside of your bed and ideally outside of your bedroom if you have the space—remember, the bed is only for sleep and sex. Finally, turn off all electronic devices 30–60 minutes before bed to allow for old-school ways to wind down that do not require screens. This will help ensure you fall asleep faster and stay asleep better.

WHEN LIFE IS JUST TOO BUSY: PRIORITIZE

Some of you may relate to this: My daughter became obsessed with the Disney movie *Frozen*. We had the hit song "Let It Go" playing on non-stop repeat in my house most evenings of the week. I learned to embrace the song's title and take it on as a mantra as best as possible. Before I had children, I prided myself on keeping a neat and clean house *all* the time, made all meals from scratch that were typically quite elaborate, and loved to take my time in the evenings to relax and unwind after the dishes were done and the kitchen was clean. When I had one child, I found it tough, but not impossible, to straighten up at the end of the day, get my son's lunch made, do the dishes and laundry (wow, babies and toddlers have a lot of laundry!), and then make time for myself for work and relaxation in the evenings. It wasn't perfect, but I was able to do it. By the time I had my daughter nearly 6 years later, my Martha Stewart ideals had to be loosened, and I am now in prioritizing mode to get through.

Gourmet dinners will happen one day, but the goal is to get everyone fed in a healthy manner as often as possible. While homemade is obviously ideal, it isn't always practical, and we must let go of any mom guilt that might be induced by perfect Facebook and Instagram pictures. Make use of delivery meal kits, grocery delivery services, frozen dinners, and premade items from the grocery store. They may cost more at times, but many healthy options are now available from which to choose. The Internet is your best friend—there are so many websites with meal planning ideas and ways to cut down on food prep time and simplify life in the kitchen. Not everything needs to be a Pinterest-worthy dinner—if it provides nourishment for you and your family, it serves its purpose. Make big batches of food using a slow cooker or pressure cooker and freeze individual portions for a later date.

Sleep need not be sacrificed for other things that can wait until tomorrow. As I sit here writing this chapter, I know that I have a pile of laundry in my den that needs to be folded and the dishwasher needs to be unloaded. However, camp bags are packed for tomorrow, lunches are made, I've allowed for an hour of writing time (with my beloved cute tortoise shell blue-blocker glasses on!), and I'm making sure I keep to my regular bedtime. I was up way later than I had planned last night, so I'm conscious of it now and not making it a pattern. Next to the basic needs for my husband and children, sleep is one of my top priorities. The dress shirts will get ironed one day, and those e-mails can wait until the next morning—what had to get done today got done, and tomorrow I'll just pick up where I left off. Sure, it makes me uncomfortable at times to see my sink full of dishes some mornings if the night just got away from me too fast. I'm working on practicing the acceptance of a hectic life, and working on being kinder to myself as I'm doing the best I can with the resources I've got. It isn't perfect, but it definitely helps to "Let It Go" each and every night. I suggest you give it a try—it is quite freeing when you put your basic needs above things that can wait a day or two. (And for when my husband reads this: He pulls his equal share in the house as well—but even with his help when he gets home, with his full-time job with a long commute and with two kids, it still all doesn't get done every night. And I'm [working on being] OK with that.)

SET LIMITS AT WORK

Work needs an end time as well. Our desire to be "on" 24/7 has been a huge player in our sleepless society and makes it even more difficult for our brains to shut off. Try to make a habit of shutting down your work computer and phone at least 2 hours before bedtime to allow for your brain to settle down and start producing melatonin. If you can't get out from under the mass of e-mails and projects piling up, come up with a list of what *must* get done tonight in order to keep your job. If you prioritize winding down and a consistent sleep/wake schedule to allow for a better night of sleep, you'll find that you will be more productive in your day-to- day work and home life. The cycle has to be broken somewhere—it isn't easy, but once you set limits it will help your overall daytime functioning.

A lot of women are afraid to speak up to their employers and ask for what they want. If you're running around from the office to home with a long commute or multiple drop-offs/pickups and are feeling run down, consider asking your boss if it would be OK to work remotely from home one or two days a week. In a lot of situations where I'm hesitant to ask for what I want, I'm a big fan of asking, "What's the worst thing that could happen?" In a case like this, really evaluate the worst-case scenario for asking for a day or two to work from home. Then ask yourself what the best-case scenario is and what the most realistic outcome is likely to be. In most instances, the best case and most realistic cases are quite similar, yet we tend to focus on the worst one. Is it likely you'll get reprimanded or fired for asking to work remotely? Unlikely, if you have been a good worker and earned respect at your job. Many employers are allowing workers to spend some time working from home given that most things can be done online or through computer-based video conferences. If you save 2 hours on your commute, twice a week, by working from home, that's extra time to make your nighttime more conducive to winding down and setting the stage for relaxation and sleep on a consistent basis.

Think of things that you could ask for from your employer to make your life a tad easier that might actually be a possibility but never dreamed of asking for in the past. You'd be surprised at what you might get. It doesn't always *have* to be so difficult. Sometimes we choose to take the most challenging of routes and do not look for other ways to alleviate our stress and make life just a little bit easier.

CHECK YOUR MOOD

Being busy does not necessarily mean that you are efficient with what you are doing. Evaluate your day to see where you may be wasting extra time and energy on things that don't really require as much emphasis as you place on them. If you're overly stressed and worried that you will never be able to catch up with all you have to do, it is possible that you might need some additional stress reduction and time management strategies, possibly even an evaluation from a psychologist, who can see if any anxiety or depression is fueling the problem. Indecisiveness, stress, irritability, sadness, hopelessness, helplessness, and racing thoughts and worries that are uncontrollable may all be signs of a bigger problem. Making the time for more in-depth evaluation and help for these issues—to see what really is an immediate genuine problem in your life and what you worry is an issue—may help bring a lot of relief.

ENLIST THE HELP OF YOUR KIDS AND PARTNER

Women also tend to take on most of the household tasks even though there's often a partner and children at home who can help out. We need to work on speaking up and asking for help, not seeing it as a weakness but instead viewing it as a strength to know our limits and assertively ask for what we need and want in our life. You are not necessarily the only one who is responsible for keeping the household running. If you have a partner at home, divide up responsibilities, for example, one does the cooking, the other does the dishes, and twice a week you do takeout. And kids can help with cleaning up toys until they're old enough to take on other household duties.

I was recently sitting with a bunch of mom friends at a children's birthday party, and we were all discussing how hectic and exhausting the mornings tend to be with getting everyone fed, dressed, and out the door to school on time. We all had 8-year-old children as well as younger kids in the house, and it dawned on me that, although I was making my son breakfasts every single morning, he could probably make some of it by himself on a regular basis. Sure, he might not be able to make the special oatmeal that I make with a mix of healthy ingredients that he doesn't quite know is in there, but the mornings he has a toaster waffle with a banana or cereal with blueberries and milk are probably mornings when he could easily make breakfast himself (and for his 2-year-old sister!) after he gets himself dressed. Taking the time one Sunday afternoon to go through a few breakfasts with him made all the difference in alleviating a little bit of my morning stress, allowing me to sleep just a few minutes later and not feel so rushed every day. Plus, he takes great pride in making breakfast for himself and his sister—I just was stuck in the rut of assuming he needed me to do these things for him even though he was in second grade. You'll be surprised at what your children can do to help out—don't assume that you have to do everything yourself.

Takeaway Message: Don't Sacrifice Sleep for Your Busy Life

- ✓ Protect your sleep/wake schedule at night and allowing time to wind down and get in bed on time should be at the top of your basic needs list.
- ✓ Making sleep a priority will benefit you and your family in the long run.

APPENDIX OF RESOURCES

Finding a Qualified Behavioral Sleep Medicine Specialist

Ideally you will find that the techniques in this book help you at least to some degree. Sometimes, though, people desire more direct guidance and someone who will hold them accountable when there's a desire to ignore the sleep rules. Clinicians who specialize in cognitive behavioral therapy for insomnia (CBT-I) are few and far between, and finding one can be challenging if you don't live in a metropolitan area. The gold standard in the field has been the Certified in Behavioral Sleep Medicine (CBSM) designation, allowing you to know that the person you see has been certified in behavioral sleep medicine by the American Academy of Sleep Medicine (the governing board in the field of sleep medicine). That being said, the certification process is being revamped to a new Diplomat in Behavioral Sleep Medicine (DBSM) certification, with the exam now governed by the Society of Behavioral Sleep Medicine. Finding someone with either a CBSM or DBSM certification will ensure the person has met strict requirements and passed an exam to practice.

However, supply doesn't match up to demand in this case. If you desire to see someone in person for CBT-I, another generally excellent option is to go to the Society of Behavioral Sleep Medicine website (www.behavioralsleep.org/). It is my understanding that providers listed there have all taken intensive training in this treatment but might not necessarily carry a CBSM or DBSM. (Of course, you need to feel comfortable with the person you are seeing, so please do not rely on my impressions but inquire about the provider's training and experience.) There are many excellent providers there to choose from. I have also been impressed by the University of Pennsylvania Behavioral Sleep Medicine Program and offers an international directory for CBT-I practitioners (www.pennsleep .directory).

Finding an Accredited Sleep Center and Board-Certified Sleep Medicine Specialist

American Academy of Sleep Medicine facility search page: http://sleep
    education.org/find-a-facility
National Sleep Foundation sleep professional locator: http://sleepfound
    foundation.clubexpress.com/content.aspx?page_id=1495&club_id=
    903482&sl=594445175

Resources for Mood Disorders, Anxiety, and Depression

Academy of Cognitive Therapy: https://www.academyofct.org
Association for Behavioral and Cognitive Therapy: http://www.abct.org
Anxiety and Depression Association of America: https://adaa.org
Burns, D. D. (1981). *Feeling good: The new mood therapy.* New York, NY:
    Penguin Books.
Clark, D. A., & Beck, A. T. (2011). *The anxiety and worry workbook: The
    cognitive behavioral solution.* New York, NY: Guilford Press.
Covey, S. R. (2013). *The seven habits of highly effective people: Powerful les-
    sons in personal change* (special ed.). New York, NY: Simon and Schuster.
Craske, M. G., & Barlow, D. H. (2006). *Mastery of your anxiety and worry
    workbook: Treatments that work.* New York, NY: Oxford University Press.
Greenberger, D., & Padesky, C. A. (1995). *Mind over mood: Change how
    you feel by changing the way you think.* New York, NY: Guilford Press.

Harris, R. (2008). *The happiness trap: How to stop struggling and start living: A guide to ACT.* Boston, MA: Trumpeter Books.

Hayes, S. C. (2005). *Get out of your mind and into your life: The new acceptance and commitment therapy.* Oakland, CA: New Harbinger.

Leahy, R. L. (2005). *The worry cure: Seven steps to stop worry from stopping you.* New York, NY: Three Rivers Press.

Leahy, R. L. (2010). *Beat the blues before they beat you: How to overcome depression.* New York, NY: Hay House.

Rego, S., & Fader, S. (2018). *The ten-step depression relief workbook: A cognitive behavioral therapy approach.* New York, NY: Althea Press.

Strosahl, K. D., & Robinson, P. J. (2008). *The mindfulness and acceptance workbook for depression: Using acceptance and commitment therapy to move through depression and create a life worth living.* Oakland, CA: New Harbinger.

Williams, M., Teasdale, J., & Segal, Z. (2007). *The mindful way through depression: Freeing yourself from chronic unhappiness.* New York, NY: Guilford Press.

Wilson, K. G., & Dufrene, T. (2010). *Things might go terribly, horribly wrong: A guide to life liberated from anxiety.* Oakland, CA: New Harbinger.

Books to Cultivate Mindfulness

Harris, D. (2014). *Ten percent happier: How I tamed the voice in my head, reduced stress without losing my edge, and found self-help that actually works—a true story.* New York, NY: HarperCollins.

Kabat-Zinn, J. (2013). *Full catastrophe living: Using the wisdom of your body and mind to face stress, pain, and illness.* New York, NY: Bantam Books.

Davis, M., Eshelman, E. R & McKay, M. (2008). *The relaxation and stress reduction workbook* (6th ed.). Oakland, CA: New Harbinger.

Stahl, B., Goldstein, E., & Santorelli, S. (2010). *A mindfulness-based stress reduction workbook.* Oakland, CA: New Harbinger.

Apps for Relaxation and Mindfulness

Many excellent apps are available to help cultivate mindfulness. Some require a paid monthly subscription with new content added on a regular basis, others are a pay-one-time fee, and others are completely free. Play around and see what works for you. They're extremely popular and people love them more and more. Remember though, they are not meant as a sedative for you! Don't use them to fall asleep with, use them to quiet your mind and be mindful of your racing brain, essentially helping you to set the stage for sleep. Here are some I've either checked out myself or heard about from people who have used them.

- Meditation Studio
- Headspace
- Calm
- Buddhify
- Insight Timer
- Smiling Mind
- The Mindfulness App
- Stop, Breathe & Think
- 10% Happier
- Breathe
- Mindfulness Bell

Books on Women's Hormonal Changes, Postpartum Issues, or Menopause

Gottfried, S. (2013). *The hormone cure: Reclaim balance, sleep and sex drive; lose weight; feel focused, vital and energized naturally with the Gottfried protocol.* New York, NY: Scribner Press.

Kantrowitz, B., & Wingert, P. (2017). *The menopause book: The complete guide* (rev. ed.). New York, NY: Workman.

Kleiman, K. R., & Raskin, V. D. (2013). *This isn't what I expected: Overcoming postpartum depression*. Boston, MA: Da Capo Press.

Northrup, C. (2006). *Women's bodies, women's wisdom: Creating physical and emotional health and healing* (rev. ed.). New York, NY: Bantam Dell.

Northrup, C. (2012) *The wisdom of menopause: Creating physical and emotional health during the change* (rev. ed.). New York, NY: Bantam Books.

Wiegartz, P. S., & Gyoerkoe, K. L. (2009). *The pregnancy and postpartum anxiety workbook: Practical skills to help you overcome anxiety, worry, panic attacks, obsessions, and compulsions*. Oakland, CA: New Harbinger.

Resources for Children's Sleep

Pediatric Sleep Council: www.babysleep.com

Huebner, D. (2008). *What to do when you dread your bed: A kid's guide to overcoming problems with sleep*. Washington, DC: Magination Press.

Mindell, J. A. (2005). *Sleeping through the night: How infants, toddlers and their parents can get a good night's sleep* (rev. ed.). New York, NY: HarperCollins.

Owens, J. A., & Mindell, J. A. (2005). *Take charge of your child's sleep: The all-in-one resource for solving sleep problems in kids and teens*. New York, NY: Marlowe.

Caring for Aging Parents

Mace, N. L., & Rabins, P. V. (2011). *The 36-hour day: A family guide to caring for people who have Alzheimer's disease, related dementias and memory loss* (5th ed.). Baltimore, MD: John's Hopkins Press.

Morris, V. (2014). *How to care for aging parents: A one-stop resource for all your medical, financial, housing and emotional issues* (3rd ed.). New York, NY: Workman.

REFERENCES

Abbasi, S., Alimohammadi, N., & Pahlavanzadeh, S. (2016). Effectiveness of cognitive behavioral therapy on the quality of sleep in women with multiple sclerosis: A randomized controlled trial study. *International Journal of Community Based Nursing and Midwifery, 4*(4), 320–328.

Abbott, S. M., Attarian, H., & Zee, P. C. (2014). Sleep disorders in perinatal women. *Best Practice and Research Clinical Obstetrics and Gynaecology, 28*(1), 159–168.

Agargun, M. Y., Kara, H., & Solmaz, M. (1997). Sleep disturbances and suicidal behavior in patients with major depression. *Journal of Clinical Psychology, 58*(6), 249–251.

Ameratunga, D., Goldin, J., & Hickey, M. (2012). Sleep disturbance in menopause. *Internal Medicine Journal, 42*(7), 742–747.

American Psychiatric Association. (2013). *Diagnostic and statistical manual of mental disorders* (5th ed.). Arlington, VA: American Psychiatric Association.

Bailey, B. W., Allen, M. D., LeCheminant, J. D., Tucker, L.A., Errico, W.K., Christensen, W.F. & Hill, M.D. (2014). Objectively measured sleep patterns in young adult women and the relationship to adiposity. *American Journal of Health Promotion, 29*(1), 46–54.

Baker, F., Zambotti, M., Colrain, I. M. & Bei, B. (2018). Sleep problems during the menopausal transition: Prevalence, impact, and the management challenges. *Nature and Science of Sleep, 10*, 73–95.

Balserak, B.I. (2015). Sleep disordered breathing in pregnancy. *Breathe, 11*, 268–77.

Baron, K. G., Abbott, S., Jao, N., Manalo, M.D. & Mullen, R. (2017). Orthosomnia: Are some patients taking the quantified self too far? *Journal of Clinical Sleep Medicine, 13*(2), 351–354.

Belanger, L., Morin, C. M., Langlois, F., & Ladouceur, R. (2004). Insomnia and generalized anxiety disorder: Effects of cognitive behavior therapy for GAD on insomnia symptoms. *Journal of Anxiety Disorders, 18*(4), 561–571.

Belleville, G., Cousineau, H., Levrier, K. & St-Pierre-Delorme, M.E. (2011). Meta-analytic review of the impact of cognitive behavior therapy for insomnia on concomant anxiety. *Clinical Psychology Review, 31*(4), 638–652.

Black, D., O'Reilly, G., Olmstead, R., Breen, E.G. & Irwin, M.R. (2015). Mindfulness meditation and improvement in sleep quality and daytime impairment among older adults with sleep disturbances: A randomized clinical trial. *JAMA Internal Medicine, 175*(4), 494–501.

Blackwell, D. (2013). Quickstats: Percentage of adults aged ≥18 years who often felt worried, nervous or anxious by sex and age group—National Health Interview Survey, United States, 2010–2011. *Morbidity and Mortality Weekly Report, 62*(10), 197.

Blom, K., Jernelov, S., Ruck, C., Lindefors, N. & Kaldo, V. (2016). Three-year follow-up of insomnia and hypnotics after controlled internet treatment for insomnia. *Sleep, 39*(6), 1267–1274.

Blumenthal, J. A., Babyak, M. A., Moore, K. A., Craighead, W.E., Herman, S., Khatri, P . . . & Krishnan, K. R. (1999). Effects of exercise training on older patients with major depression. *Archives of Internal Medicine, 159*(19), 2349–2356.

Bootzin, R. R. (1972). Stimulus control treatment for insomnia. *Proceedings of the 80th Annual Meeting of the American Psychological Association, 7,* 395–396.

Bootzin, R. R., & Perlis, M. L. (1992). Nonpharmacologic treatments of insomnia. *Journal of Clinical Psychiatry, 53(Suppl.),* 37–41.

Borbely, A. A. (1982). A two process model of sleep regulation. *Human Neurobiology, 1(3),* 195–204.

Borbely, A. A., Daan, S., Wirz-Justice, A. & Deboer, T. (2016). The two-process model of sleep regulation: A reappraisal. *Journal of Sleep Research, 25(2),* 131–143.

Brasure, M., Fuchs, E., MacDonald, R., Nelson, V.A., Koffel, E., Olson, C.M . . . . & Kane, R.L. (2016). Psychological and behavioral interventions for managing insomnia disorder: An evidence report for a clinical practice guideline by the American College of Physicians. *Annals of Internal Medicine, 165(2),* 113–124.

Carney, C. E., Edinger, J. D., Kuchibhatla, M. Lachowski, A.M., Bogouslavsky, O., Krystal, A.D. & Shapiro, C.M. (2017). Cognitive behavioral insomnia therapy for those with insomnia and depression: A randomized controlled clinical trial. *Sleep, 40(4),* zsx019.

Carney, C. E., Segal., Z. V., Edinger, J. D. & Krystal, A.D. (2007). A comparison of rates of residual insomnia symptoms following pharmacotherapy or cognitive behavioral therapy for major depressive disorder. *Journal of Clinical Psychology, 68(2),* 254–260.

Chang, A., Aeschback, D., Duffy, J., & Czeisler, C.A. (2015). Evening use of light-emitting eReaders negatively affects sleep, circadian timing and next-morning alertness. *Proceedings of the National Academy of Sciences of the U. S. A., 112(4),* 1232–1237.

Chung, K., Lee, C., Yeung, W., Chan, M.S., Chung, E.W. & Lin, W.L. (2017). Sleep hygiene education as a treatment of insomnia: A systematic review and meta-analysis. *Family Practice,* 1–11.

Ciano, C., King, T. S., Wright, R. R., Perlis, M. & Sawyer, A.M. (2017). Longitudinal study of insomnia symptoms among women during perimenopause. *Journal of Obstetric, Gynecologic, and Neonatal Nursing, 46*(6), 804–813.

Currie, S. R., Wilson, K. G., Pontefract, A. J., et al. (2000). Cognitive-behavioral treatment of insomnia secondary to chronic pain. *Journal of Consulting and Clinical Psychology, 68,* 407–416.

Davidson, J. R. (2009). Insomnia treatment options for women. *Obstetrics and Gynecology Clinics of North America, 36*(4), 831–84 6.

Davidson, J. R., Waisberg, J.L., Brundage, M.D. & MacLean, A.W. (2001). Nonpharmacologic group treatment of insomnia: A preliminary study with cancer survivors. *Psycho-Oncology, 10,* 389–397.

Duffy, J. F., Cain, S. W., Chang, A., Phillips, A.J., Munch, M.Y., Gronifer, C . . . & Czeisler, C.a. (2011). Sex difference in the near-24-hour intrinsic period of the human circadian timing system. *Proceedings of the National Academy of Sciences of the U. S. A., 13*(108), 15602–15608.

Edinger, J. D., Olsen, M. K., Stechuchak, K. M., Means, M.K., Lineberger, M.D., Kirby, A. & Carney, C.E. (2009). Cognitive behavioral therapy for patients with primary insomnia or insomnia associated predominantly with mixed psychiatric disorders: A randomized clinical trial. *Sleep, 32*(4), 499–510.

Espie, C. A., Fleming, L., Cassidy, J., Samuel, L., Taylor, L.M., White, C.A . . . . & Paul, J. (2008). Randomized controlled clinical effectiveness trial of cognitive behavior therapy compared with treatment as usual for persistent insomnia in patients with cancer. *Journal of Clinical Oncology, 26,* 4651–4658.

Exelmans, L., & Van den Bulck, J. (2017). Binge viewing, sleep and the role of pre-sleep arousal. *Journal of Clinical Sleep Medicine, 13*(8), 1001–1008.

Fernandez, R. C., Moore, V. M., Van Ryswyk, E. M., Varcoe, T.J., Rodgers, R.J., March, W.A . . . & Davies, M.J. (2018). Sleep disturbances in women with polycystic ovary syndrome: Prevalence, pathophysiology, impact and management strategies. *Nature and Science of Sleep, 10,* 45–64.

Ford, D. E., & Kamerow, D. B. (1989). Epidemiologic study of sleep disturbances in psychiatric disorders: An opportunity for prevention? *JAMA, 262*(11), 1479–1484.

Franklin, K. A., Sablin, C., Stenlund, H., et al. (2013). Sleep apnoea is a common occurrence in females. *European Respiratory Journal, 41*(3), 610–615.

Freedman, R. R. (2014). Menopausal hot flashes: Mechanisms, endocrinology, treatment. *Journal of Steroid Biochemistry and Molecular Biology, 142*, 115–120.

Gong, H., Ni, C., Liu, Z., Zhang, Y., Su, W.J. LIzn, Y.J . . . & Jiang, C.L. (2016). Mindfulness meditation for insomnia: A meta-analysis of randomized controlled trials. *Journal of Psychosomatic Research, 89*, 1–6.

Goyal, M., Singh, S., Sibinga, E. M., Gould, N.F., Rowland-Seymour, A., Sharma, R . . . & Haythornthwaite, J.A. (2014). Meditation for psychological stress and well-being: A systematic review and meta-analysis. *JAMA Internal Medicine, 174*(3), 357–368.

Gray, S.L., Anderson, M.L., Dublin, S., Hanlon, J.T., Hubbard, R., Walker, R . . . & Larson, E.B. (2015). Cumulative use of strong anticholinergics and inicident dementia: a prospective cohort study. *JAMA Intern Med, 175*(3), 401–7.

Gross, C. R., Kreitzer, M. J., Reilly-Spong, M., Wall, M., Winbush, N.Y., Patterson, R . . . & Cramer-Bornemann, M. (2011). Mindfulness-based stress reduction versus pharmacotherapy for chronic primary insomnia: A randomized controlled clinical trial. *Explore (New York), 7*(2), 76–87.

Hall, M. H., Matthews, K. A., & Kravitz, H. M. (2009). Race and financial strain are independent correlates of sleep in midlife women: The SWAN sleep study. *Sleep, 32*(1), 73–82.

Holqvist, M., Vincent, N., & Walsh, K. (2014). Web- vs. telehealth-based delivery of cognitive behavioral therapy for insomnia: A randomized controlled trial. *Sleep Medicine, 15*(2), 187–195.

Home, J. A., & Reid, A. J. (1985). Night-time sleep EEG changes following body heating in a warm bath. *Electroencephalography and Clinical Neurophysiology, 60*(2), 154–157.

Jacobs, G. D., Pace-Schott, E. F., Stickgold, R. & Otto, M.W. (2004). Cognitive behavioral therapy and pharmacotherapy for insomnia: A randomized controlled trial and direct comparison. *Archives of Internal Medicine, 164*(17), 1888–1896.

Joffe, H., Massler, A., & Sharkey, K. M. (2010). Evaluation and management of sleep disturbance during the menopause transition. *Seminars in Reproductive Medicine, 28*(5), 404–421.

Jungquist, C. R., O'Brien, C., Matteson-Rusby, S., Smith, M.T., Pigeon, W.R., Xia, Y . . . & Perlis, M.L. (2010). The efficacy of cognitive-behavioral therapy for insomnia in patients with chronic pain. *Sleep Medicine, 11*(3), 302–309.

Kabat-Zinn, J. (2013). *Full catastrophe living: Using the wisdom of your body and mind to face stress, pain and illness.* New York, NY: Bantam Books.

Kaplan, K. A., & Harvey, A. G. (2013). Behavioral treatment of insomnia in bipolar disorder. *American Journal of Psychiatry, 170*(7), 716–720.

Ko, Y., & Lee, J. Y. (2018). Effects of feet warming using bed socks on sleep quality and thermoregulatory responses in a cool environment. *Journal of Physiological Anthropology, 37*(1), 13.

Kravitz, H. M., Ganz, P. A., Bromberger, J., Powell, L.H., Sutton-Tyrrell, K. & Meyer, P.M. (2003). Sleep difficulty in women at midlife: A community survey of sleep and the menopausal transition. *Menopause, 10*(1), 19–28.

Krishnan, V., & Collop, N. A. (2006). Gender differences in sleep disorders. *Current Opinion in Pulmonary Medicine, 12*(6), 383–9.

Liao, W. C. (2002). Effects of passive body heating on body temperature and sleep regulation in the elderly: A systematic review. *International Journal of Nursing Studies, 39*(8), 803–810.

Liao, W. C., Wang, L., Kuo, C. P., Lo, C., Chiu, M.J. & Ting, H. (2013). Effect of a warm footbath before bedtime on body temperature and sleep in older adults with good and poor sleep: An experimental cross-over trial. *International Journal of Nursing Studies, 50*(12), 1607–1616.

Mallampalli, M. P., & Carter, C. L. (2014). Exploring sex and gender differences in sleep health: A society for women's health research report. *Journal of Women's Health, 23*(7), 553–562.

Manber, R., Edinger, J. D., Gress, J. L., San Pedro-Salcedo, M.G., Kuo, T.F. & Kalista, T. (2008). Cognitive behavioral therapy for insomnia enhances depression outcome in patients with comorbid major depressive disorder and insomnia. *Sleep, 31*, 489–495.

McCurry, S., Guthrie, K., Morin, C., Woods, N.F., Landis, C.A., Ensrud, K.E . . . & LaCroix, A.Z. (2016). Telephone delivered cognitive-behavior therapy for insomnia in midlife women with vasomotor symptoms: An MsFLASH randomized trial. *JAMA Internal Medicine, 176*(7), 913–920.

McGowan, S., & Behar, E. (2013). A preliminary investigation of stimulus control training for worry: Effects on anxiety and insomnia. *Behavior Modification, 37*(1), 90–112.

Meaklim, H., & Cunnington, D. (2018). Web-based cognitive behavior therapy for insomnia shows long-term efficacy in improving chronic insomnia. *Evidence-Based Mental Health, 21*(1), e3.

Mellor, A., Stewart, E. M., Jenkins, M. M., Hamill, K., Norton, P.J., Baucom, D.M. & Drummond, S.P. (2017). Bed partner accommodation of insomnia in treatment-seeking couples. *Sleep, 40*(*Suppl.* 1), A142.

Mitchel, M. D., Gehrman, P., Perlis, M., & Umscheid, C. A. (2012). Comparative effectiveness of cognitive behavioral therapy for insomnia: A systematic review. *BMC Family Practice, 13*, 40.

Morgenthaler, T., Kramer, M., Alessi, C., Friedman, L., Boehlecke, B., Brown, T . . . & American Academy of Sleep Medicine (2006). Practice parameters for the psychological and behavioral treatment of insomnia: An update. An American Academy of Sleep Medicine Report. *Sleep, 29*(11), 1415–1419.

Morin, C. M., Beaulieu-Bonneau, S., Belanger, L., Ivers, H., Sanchez Ortuno, M., Vallieres, A . . . & Merette, C. (2016). Cognitive-behavior therapy singly and combined with medication for persistent insomnia: Impact on psychological and daytime functioning. *Behavior Research and Therapy, 87,* 109–116.

Morin, C. M., Bootzin, R. R., Buysse, D., Edinger, J.D., Espie, C.A. & Lichstein, K.L. (2006). Psychological and behavioral treatment of insomnia: Update of the recent evidence (1998–2004). *Sleep, 29*(11), 1398–1414.

Morin, C. M., Colecchi, C., Stone, J., Sood, R., Bring, D. (1999). Behavioral and pharmacological therapies for late-life insomnia: A randomized controlled trial. *JAMA, 281*(11), 991–999.

Morin, C. M., Vallieres, A., Guay, Ivers, H., Savard, J., Merette, C . . . & Baillargeon, L. (2009). Cognitive-behavior therapy, singly and combined with medication for persistent insomnia: Acute and maintenance therapeutic effects. *JAMA, 301*(19), 2005–2015.

Nappi, C. M., Drummond, S. P. A., & Hall, J. M. H. (2012). Treating nightmares and insomnia in posttraumatic stress disorder: A review of current evidence. *Neuropharmacology, 62,* 576–585.

National Institutes of Health. (2005). NIH State-of-the-Science Conference Statement on manifestations and management of chronic insomnia in adults. *NIH Consensus and State-of-the-Science Statements, 22*(2), 1–30.

Nedeltcheva, A. V., Kilkus, J. M., Imperial, J., Schoeller, D.A. & Penev, P.D. (2010). Insufficient sleep undermines dietary efforts to reduce adiposity. *Annals of Internal Medicine, 5*(7), 435–441.

Offer, S., & Schneider, B. (2011). Revisiting the gender gap in time-use patterns: Multitasking and well-being among mothers and fathers in dual-earner families. *American Sociological Review, 76*(6), 809–833.

Okajima, I., Komada, Y., & Inoue, Y. (2010). A meta-analysis on the treatment effectiveness of cognitive behavioral therapy for primary insomnia. *Sleep and Biological Rhythms, 9*(1), 24–34.

Ong, J. C., Manber, R., Segal, Z., Xia, Y., Shapiro, S. & Wyatt, J. (2014). A randomized controlled trial of mindfulness meditation for chronic insomnia. *Sleep, 37*(9), 1553–1563.

Ong, J. C., Shapiro, R., & Manber, R. (2008). Combining mindfulness meditation with cognitive-behavior therapy for insomnia: A treatment-development study. *Behavioral Therapy, 39*(2), 171–182.

Ong, J. C., Shapiro, S. L., Manber, R. (2009). Mindfulness meditation and cognitive behavioral therapy for insomnia: A naturalistic 12-month follow-up. *Explore (New York), 5*(1), 30–36.

Ong, J., & Sholtes, D. (2010). A mindfulness-based approach to the treatment of insomnia. *Journal of Clinical Psychology, 66*(11), 1175–1184.

Ophir, E., Nass, C., & Wagner, A. D. (2009). Cognitive control in media multitaskers. *Proceedings of the National Academy of Scineces of the United States of America, 106*(37), 15583–15587.

Perlis, M. L., Giles, D. E., Buysse, D. J., Tu, X. & Kupfer, D.J. (1997). Self-reported sleep disturbance as a prodromal symptom in recurrent depression. *Journal of Affective Disorders, 42*(2–3), 209–212.

Perlis, M. L., Sharpe, M., Smith, M. T., Greenblatt, D. & Giles, D. (2001). Behavioral treatment of insomnia: Treatment outcome and the relevance of medical and psychiatric morbidity. *Journal of Behavioral Medicine, 24*, 281–296.

Pollan, M. (2008). *In defense of food: An eater's manifesto.* New York, NY: Penguin Press.

Quaseem, A., Kansagara, D., Forciea, M. A., Cooke, M., & Denberg, T.D. (2016). Management of chronic insomnia disorder in adults: A clinical practice guideline. *Annals of Internal Medicine, 165*(2), 125–133.

Reimann, D., & Perlis, M. (2009). The treatments of chronic insomnia: A review of benzodiazepine receptor agonists and psychological and behavioral therapies. *Sleep Medicine Review, 13*(3), 205–214.

Reynolds, C. F., III, & Kupfer, D. J. (1987). Sleep research in affective illness: State of the art circa 1987. *Sleep, 10*(3), 199–215.

Ritterband, L. M., Thorndike, F. P., Ingersoll, K. S., Lord, H.R., Gonder-

Frederick, L., Frederick, C . . . & Morin, C.M. (2017). Effect of a Web-based cognitive behavior therapy for insomnia intervention with 1-year follow-up: A randomized clinical trial. *JAMA Psychiatry, 74*(1), 68–75.

Rossouw, J.E., Anderson, G.L., Prentice, R.L., LaCroix, A.Z., Kooperberg, C., Stefanick, M.L . . . & Ockene, J. (2002). Risks and benefits of estrogen plus progestin in healthy postmenopausal women: principal results from the Women's Health Initiative randomized controlled trial. *JAMA, 288*(3), 321–33.

Roy-Byrne, P. P., Uhde, T. W., & Post, R. M. (1986). Effects of one night's sleep deprivation on mood and behavior in panic disorder: Patients with panic disorder compared with depressed patients and normal controls. *Archives of General Psychiatry, 43*(9), 895–899.

Santoro, N. (2005). The menopausal transition. *American Journal of Medicine, 118*(Suppl. 12B), 8–13.

Schutte-Rodin, S., Broch, L., Buysse, D., Dorsey, C. & Sateia, M. (2008). Clinical guideline for the evaluation and management of chronic insomnia in adults. *Journal of Clinical Sleep Medicine 4*(5), 487–504.

Sedov, I. D., Goodman, S. H., & Tomfohr-Madsen, L. M. (2017). Insomnia treatment preferences during pregnancy. *Journal of Obstetric, Gynecologic, and Neonatal Nursing, 46*(3), e95–e104.

Segal, Z. V., Williams, J. M. G., & Teasdale, J. D. (2002). *Mindfulness-based cognitive therapy for depression: A new approach to preventing relapse.* New York, NY: Guilford Press.

Seyffert, M., Legisetty, P., Landgraf, J. Chopra, V., Pfeiffer, P.N., Conte, M.L. & Rogers, M.A. (2016). Internet-delivered cognitive behavioral therapy to treat insomnia: A systematic review and meta-analysis. *PLoS One, 11*(2), e0149139.

Shapiro, S. L., Bootzin, R. R., Figueredo, A. J., Lopez, A.M. & Schwartz, G.E. (2003). The efficacy of mindfulness-based stress reduction in the treatment of sleep disturbance in women with breast cancer: An exploratory study. *Journal of Psychosomatic Research, 54*, 85–91.

Sharkey, K. M. (2013). Time to treat problematic sleep disturbance in perinatal women. *Behavioral Sleep Medicine, 11,* 4.

Siversten, B., Omvik, S., Pallesen, S., Bjorvatn, B., Havik, O.E., Kvale, G., Nielsen, G.H. & Nordhus, I.H. (2006). Cognitive behavioral therapy vs zopiclone for treatment of chronic primary insomnia in older adults: A randomized controlled trial. *JAMA, 295*(24), 2851–2858.

Smith, M. T., Huang, M. I., & Manber, R. (2005). Cognitive behavior therapy for chronic insomnia occurring within the context of medical and psychiatric disorders. *Clinical Psychology Review, 25,* 559–592.

Smith, M. T., Perlis, M. L., Park, A., Smith, M.S., Pennington, J., Giles, D.E. & Buysse, D.J. (2002). Comparative meta-analysis of pharmacotherapy and behavior therapy for persistent insomnia. *American Journal of Psychiatry, 159*(1), 5–11.

Smitherman, T. A., Kuka, A. J., Calhoun, A. H., Walters, A.B.P., Davis-Martin, R.E., Ambrose, C.E . . . & Houle, T.T. (2018). Cognitive-behavioral therapy for insomnia to reduce chronic migraine: A sequential Bayesian analysis. *Headache, 58*(7), 1052–1059.

Spielman, A. J., & Glovinsky, P. (1991). The varied nature of insomnia. In P. J. Hauri (Ed.), *Case studies in insomnia* (pp. 1–15). New York Plenum Press.

Spielman, A. J., Saskin, P., & Thorpy, M. J. (1987). Treatment of chronic insomnia by restriction of time in bed. *Sleep, 10*(1), 45–56.

Stathopoulou, G., Powers, M. B., Berry, A. C., Smits, J.A. & Otto, M.W. (2006). Exercise interventions for mental health: A quantitative and qualitative review. *Clinical Psychology Science and Practice, 13*(2), 179–193.

Stoet, G., O'Connor, D., Conner, M. Laws, K.R. (2013). Are women better than men at multi-tasking? *BMC Psychology, 1,* 18.

Swanson, L. M., Flynn, H., Adams-Mundy, J. D. Armitage, R. & Arnedt, J.T. (2013). An open pilot of cognitive-behavioral therapy for insomnia in women with postpartum depression. *Behavioral Sleep Medicine, 11*(4), 297–307.

Taylor, D. J., Lichstein, K. L., Durence, H. H., Reidel, B.W. & Bush, A.J. (2005). Epidemiology of insomnia, depression and anxiety. *Sleep,* 28(11), 1457–1464.

Tomfohr-Madseon, L. M., Clayborne, Z. M., Rouleau, C. R. & Campbell, T.S. (2017). Sleeping for two: An open-pilot study of cognitive behavioral therapy for insomnia in pregnancy. *Behavioral Sleep Medicine,* 15(5), 377–393.

Toth, C. M. (2010). The anxious sleeper: Initiate sleep-restriction and stimulus-control techniques. *Journal of Clinical Sleep Medicine,* 6(4), 403–404.

Trauer, J. M., Chian, M. Y., Doyle, J. S., Rajaratnam, S.M. & Cunnington, D. (2015). Cognitive behavioral therapy for chronic insomnia: A systematic review and meta-analysis. *Annals of Internal Medicine,* 163(3), 191–204.

Vahratian, A. (2017). Sleep duration and quality among women aged 40–59, by menopausal status. *NCHS Data Brief 286.* Hyattsville, MD: National Center for Health Statistics.

Van Straten, A., van der Zweerde, T., Kleiboer, A., Cuijpers, P., Morin, C.M. & Lancee, J. (2018). Cognitive behavioral therapies in the treatment of insomnia: A meta-analysis. *Sleep Medicine Reviews, 38,* 3–16.

Vitiello, M. V., Rybarcyzk, B., Von Korff, M. & Stepanski, E.J. (2009). Cognitive behavioral therapy for insomnia improves sleep and decreases pain in older adults with co-morbid insomnia and osteoarthritis. *Journal of Clinical Sleep Medicine, 5,* 355–362.

Wu, J. Q., Appleman, E. R., Salazar, R. D. & Ong, J.C. (2015). Cognitive behavioral therapy for insomnia comorbid with psychiatric and medical conditions: A meta-analysis. *JAMA Internal Med, 175*(9): 1461–72.

Wu, R., Bao, J., Zhang, C., Deng, J. & Long, C. (2006). Comparison of sleep condition and sleep-related psychological activity after cognitive-behavior and pharmacological therapy for insomnia. *Psychotherapy and Psychosomatics, 75*(4), 220–228.

Xie, L., Kang, H., Xu, Q. Chen, M.J., Liao, Y., Thiyagarajan, M . . . &

Nedergaard, M. (2013). Sleep drives metabolite clearance from the adult brain. *Science, 342*(6), 373–377.

Xu, Q., & Lang, C. P. (2014). Examining the relationship between subjective sleep disturbance and menopause: A systematic review and meta-analysis. *Menopause, 21*(12), 1301–1318.

Zeyfert, C., & DeViva., J. C. (2004). Residual insomnia following cognitive behavioral therapy for PTSD. *Journal of Traumatic Stress, 17*(1), 69–73.

Zhang, B., & Wing, Y. K. (2006). Sex differences in insomnia: A meta-analysis. *Sleep, 29*(1), 85–93.

INDEX

ABOUT THE AUTHOR

Shelby Harris, Psy.D., is in private practice in White Plains, NY where she specializes in the use of Cognitive Behavior Therapy (CBT) for anxiety and depression. She is board certified in Behavioral Sleep Medicine (BSM) by the American Academy of Sleep Medicine and treats a wide variety of sleep disorders (insomnia, nightmares, circadian rhythm disorders, narcolepsy, apnea treatment noncompliance) using evidence-based non-pharmacological treatments. Before going into private practice, Dr. Harris was the longstanding director of the Behavioral Sleep Medicine Program at the Sleep-Wake Disorders Center at Montefiore Medical Center.

Dr. Harris currently holds a dual academic appointment as Clinical Associate Professor at the Albert Einstein College of Medicine in both the Neurology and Psychiatry Departments. Dr. Harris has published and presented research on the neuropsychological effects of insomnia in older adults as well as behavioral treatments for insomnia, parasomnias, narcolepsy, and excessive daytime sleepiness. She is frequently invited by hospitals and organizations to give grand rounds lectures and workshops.

She obtained her undergraduate degree with honors from Brown University and graduated with her doctorate in clinical psychology from the Ferkauf Graduate School of Psychology, Yeshiva University. Dr. Harris completed her predoctoral internship at Montefiore Medical Center where she trained in the Sleep-Wake Disorders Center and received advanced postdoctoral training in Cognitive Behavior Therapy for anxiety and depression.

Dr. Harris has been an invited columnist for *The New York Times* "Consults Blog," Dr. Oz's website "You Beauty," and Psychology Today and is frequently quoted in the media, including such publications as *The New York Times, The Huffington Post, The New Yorker, Wall Street Journal,* and *New York Magazine.* She has appeared on *The Today Show, World News with Diane Sawyer, Good Morning America,* ABC7-NY's Eyewitness News, CBS News, and ABC's Primetime: Live.